5 STEPS FOR SELECTING THE BEST FINANCIAL ADVISOR

5 STEPS

for

SELECTING

The Best Financial Advisor|

How the Internet
Has Changed the Game
For Investors
and Financial Advisors

Jack Waymire & Jonathan Dash

A SEQUEL TO *WHO'S WATCHING YOUR MONEY?*

PALADIN PUBLISHING

5 STEPS FOR SELECTING THE BEST FINANCIAL ADVISOR
How the Internet Has Changed the Game
for Investors and Financial Advisors

ISBN 978-1-5445-0067-6 *Hardcover*
    978-1-5445-0065-2 *Paperback*
    978-1-5445-0066-9 *Ebook*
    978-1-5445-0068-3 *Audiobook*

CONTENTS

ACKNOWLEDGMENTS

We would like to acknowledge the valuable input and assistance of several people who helped us research, write, and edit this book. In particular, we would like to thank Richard Best, who was very involved in the writing of the book. His research also made valuable additions to the quality of the final version of the book. We would also like to thank Debbie Freeman, Steve Ray, Susan Bishop, and Jamie Johnston for their feedback and contributions.

INTRODUCTION

When I wrote *Who's Watching Your Money?* (2000–2002), the stock market was in a major tailspin that would ultimately cost investors $8 trillion in realized and unrealized losses. Investors, who had been riding the 1990s boom for tech, dot-com, and communications stocks, were stunned when their retirement and savings accounts were devastated by losses of 50 percent or more. Millions of investors spent years recovering losses only to be hit again by the toxic mortgage meltdown that triggered the 2008 stock market crash and another $12 trillion of realized and unrealized losses.

I remember one friend in particular who spent eighteen years in the banking industry accumulating retirement assets in her company's 401(k) plan. She decided to join another bank in 1999 and felt relieved when a Dean Witter (now Morgan Stanley) branch manager agreed to invest the retirement assets she had rolled into an IRA. The manager recommended several proprietary Dean Witter mutual funds that were heavily invested in technology-related stocks. She left the meeting feeling her financial future was in good hands. After all, Dean Witter was a brand name, the branch manager was an experienced professional, and their slogan sounded right: "We measure success one investor at a time."

However, when the dust settled after the 2000–2002 stock market crash, she had lost 65 percent of her retirement savings. Retirement was no longer a realistic option. She would have to work another ten to fifteen years to recover her losses. In the meantime, the branch manager had pocketed some sizable commissions, and Dean Witter had deducted thousands of dollars of expenses from her assets.

It was painfully obvious that her losses were more than they should have been because she selected the wrong financial advisor.

I decided to write my first book after hearing story after story that described how bad financial advice had made bad stock market returns even worse. However,

I was also realistic. I knew there was nothing I could write that would impact the business practices of the firms that make up the industry we call Wall Street.

I concluded that if this book was going to help investors protect their financial interests, the emphasis had to be on their selection of financial advisors. You and I can't change Wall Street business practices, but we can change the way we pick financial advisors.

You have to control the process for selecting your financial advisor. If you don't control the process, the advisors will.

THE NEXT BUBBLE

As of the writing of this book, we have had several years of positive stock market returns, so there is a good chance you are satisfied with your current advisor. We have three warnings that make the content in this book relevant and timely.

First, do not assume the stock market will go up forever. This assumption resulted in trillions of dollars of losses in 2000–2002 and 2008.

Second, you may be giving your advisor credit for the recent performance of the stock market. Your current advisor may not be as knowledgeable as you think he is.

Third, the real expertise of an advisor is determined in down markets when his role is to minimize your losses.

SELECTING ADVISORS

Wall Street is counting on your not knowing much about financial planning and investment principles. This general lack of knowledge creates the need for financial advisors. It also opens the door to advisors who use sales skills to represent themselves as financial experts.

An expert can be someone who knows a little more about a topic than you do.

You need a financial advisor for the same reasons you hire CPAs and attorneys. You do not have the time, specialized knowledge, or inclination to do the work yourself. But you don't want just any advisor. You want a competent, ethical professional who puts your financial interests first.

Select the right advisor, and you should have more money in the future. Select the wrong advisor, and there is a good chance you will have less money. Consequently, this is one of the most important financial decisions that you will ever make. It is also one of the riskiest.

Why risky? You are up against the Wall Street marketing machine.

THE MARKETING MACHINE

Wall Street wants to make your financial advisor selection process a subjective, sales process.

It is a lot easier to create a skilled salesperson (a few weeks) than a financial expert (several years). Wall Street wants new advisors producing revenue in weeks, not years.

This strategy has worked for more than fifty years because the only way you could learn more about advisors was to talk to them. They controlled most of the information you needed to make your selection decision, which also created the opportunity for their sales pitches. Consequently, you were more likely to select the advisor with the best personality or sales pitch versus the advisor with the best qualifications.

This book will teach you how to develop a process that you can use to select the best financial advisor for the right reasons.

WALL STREET'S MYSTIQUE

A remarkable study conducted by Harvard academics

in 2008, just six years after the previous stock market crash and shortly before the next one, illustrated the tactics of the Wall Street marketing machine.

A research team sent a group of "mystery shoppers" into the offices of 284 financial advisors in the Boston area seeking advice on how to invest retirement savings outside of their 401(k) plans. They showed the advisors a diversified portfolio of low-cost, passive index funds and asked them for an opinion about this strategy. Just 2.4 percent of the advisors provided positive feedback. Nearly 85 percent recommended changing the portfolio to higher-cost, actively managed funds that produced increased revenue for their firms and more income for them.

This should not have been a big surprise. The advisors had to recommend changes to produce revenue and income.

However, what happened next was even scarier. Seventy percent of the shoppers said they liked the advisors so much that they would follow their investment recommendations even though the expenses would be substantially higher and there was no guarantee that results would be better. This is a scary illustration of the influence that Wall Street's sales force has over investors.

Wall Street knows people inherently trust people they like. Advisor personalities are a powerful marketing tool.

We did not write this book to bash Wall Street and its marketing practices. However, it is important that you know Wall Street is a powerful adversary when you are trying to do what is best for you while Wall Street is trying to do what is best for firms and advisors.

That is why we decided to write this book. We wanted to create a level playing field for investors who relied on the advice and services of financial advisors.

THE INTERNET CHANGES THE GAME

We live and work in an information-based society. Does it make any sense to base your financial advisor selection decisions on sales pitches?

How can you level the playing field so you make the "right" decision when you select a financial advisor? And how about making a "safer" decision that reduces your risk of selecting the wrong advisor? The answer is at your fingertips!

You already know that you live in an age where you can find just about anything you want to know on the internet. You just have to know where to go to find the information, and you have to understand the importance of what you find.

Using the internet to research financial advisors is not a new or revolutionary idea. What is new is using the internet to control a process that helps you make the right decision when you select a financial advisor.

You are no longer limited to the information that advisors provide you in their sales pitches. When advisors control information, you hear what they want you to hear. It is also easy to manipulate information with misrepresentation and omission because there is no written record of what was said to you.

The internet provides a level of transparency that is still relatively new to an industry that is used to controlling the information you rely on to select financial advisors.

WHO ARE THE BEST FINANCIAL ADVISORS?

This is the mystery that the internet will help you solve. Yes, it is going to take a little time on your part, but a little effort now can pay big dividends later.

There are more than six hundred thousand advisors and registered representatives in the United States who sell financial advice, services, and products. Every major city in America has thousands of advisors who purport to be trustworthy financial experts. However, after years of experience researching advisors, we can tell you that many are not. Approximately 25 percent of these advisors are real experts. At least 50 percent are salespeople. The remaining 25 percent are in transition from selling to advising.

Your challenge is to select a trustworthy advisor who can provide high-quality advice that helps you achieve your financial goals.

SELECT THE BEST

This book will show you how to control the process you use for selecting the best financial advisor—by using the internet to find qualified professionals and thoroughly researching them before you contact them. Plus, the internet allows you to retain your anonymity while you find and learn more about particular advisors.

You will learn which websites publish the information you need, and you will know the difference between information that benefits you and information that may contain hidden risks.

You will also learn how to use the internet to validate

the information that advisors provide to you during interviews.

You win when you control the process—and when you select the best financial advisor for the right reasons.

We may not be able to change the business practices of Wall Street, but the information and tools in this book can empower you to change how you select your next or first financial advisor.

CHAPTER 1

HOW TO AVOID THE NEXT BERNIE MADOFF

Eleven thousand investors could have used the internet to avoid the biggest investment scam in US history!

When Bernie Madoff was arrested in December 2008, he instantly became the face of the greed and corruption that has permeated Wall Street for decades. It is common knowledge that he bilked eleven thousand investors out of $65 billion in the largest and most damaging Ponzi scheme in history. Madoff pleaded guilty to multiple counts of fraud, theft, and money laundering and was sentenced to 150 years in prison.

How bad were the consequences of his criminal enterprise? There were thousands of victims, suicides, and multiple bankruptcies. Less than $12 billion has been recovered for Madoff victims, many of whom lost all or a significant portion of their wealth.

We say "wealth" because it was not as if Madoff's victims were unsophisticated people who invested small amounts of money in his scheme. Most of Madoff's victims were wealthy people and institutions—millionaires, celebrities, executives, banks, European royalty, pension funds, university endowments, charitable foundations, and hedge fund managers—all of whom felt privileged to have their assets invested by a "Wall Street Wizard" who had the Midas touch.

IT CAN HAPPEN AGAIN

Why lead off with Bernie Madoff? After all, this happened years ago and is old news. We hope his story is an attention-getter for the following reasons:

- History can repeat itself, even if it is not as dramatic.
- Bad financial advice is still bad advice.
- There are very few Madoffs, but there are thousands of bad advisors.
- He had current industry licenses while he stole from his clients.

- His victims could have avoided him with a few minutes of online research.

THE ALLURE OF BERNIE MADOFF

Madoff managed to engineer an "Oz" persona—he was the evil genius behind the curtain who rarely met face-to-face with his clients. But that didn't matter as long as he delivered the consistent 10–12 percent returns that he promised them.

The lie he inserted into his sales pitch was that he could deliver good (not great) returns regardless of market conditions. It turned out the claim was too good to be true.

No one dared question his methods or results because they were afraid he would drop them from his list of wealthy clientele. He even turned away some investors to create a sense of exclusivity, which made him even more alluring to the rich and famous. Although he guaranteed easy access to their funds, his clients were afraid to withdraw their money for fear of not being able to get back in.

His clients were not stupid people. They had to accumulate a lot of assets just to afford his investment services. Plus, they were surrounded by tax, legal, and financial specialists who were supposed to protect their interests.

The Madoff story was a finely honed blend of fact and fiction. He founded one of the largest market makers on Wall Street. He served as the chairman of the Board of Directors for the National Association of Securities Dealers (NASD), the then self-regulatory body for the securities industry. He was a member of the Board of Directors of the Securities Industry Association, which wielded a substantial amount of political power in Washington, DC. Obviously, he was a man who could be trusted by virtue of his industry visibility, past accomplishments, and sterling credentials.

He was also very charming. Like many of the best con artists, he was an exceptional schmoozer, with an uncanny ability to convince wealthy individuals that he had a unique process for investing their assets. Not only was he able to convince people he could produce positive returns in all market conditions, but he made them feel exceptionally lucky to be investing with him.

One of the most frequent laments from his victims was: "I thought he was my friend."

THE EASY DECISION

When in the presence of a person with this amount of charisma, most people feel awkward even asking questions—they just hand over their money and hope he is as good as people say he is.

His victims bought the story, so there was no need to spend valuable time researching someone who appeared to have mastered the art of walking on water. How do you question the claims of an advisor when everyone you've talked to has said he made good on his promises?

THE DOWNFALL (2008)

No one can pinpoint exactly when Madoff decided to become a criminal and launch his scam, but the authorities assumed he had been running it for at least fifteen years before he turned himself in. Like most Ponzi schemes, the scam collapsed when too many investors wanted to pull all or part of their money out of the market and there was not enough new money to fund the withdrawals.

Funding withdrawals had not been a problem for Madoff until late 2008, at the peak of the most recent financial meltdown, when several clients simultaneously wanted to withdraw almost $7 billion. At that point, Madoff had less than $300 million in available assets. His scam was finally over. Madoff revealed his deception to his sons who worked at his firm. His sons went to the authorities, and Madoff was led away in handcuffs.

FIGHTING OUR OWN DEMONS

To this day, the image of Bernie Madoff in handcuffs serves as a warning to all investors. While we may never see anything on the scale of the Madoff scam again, there is still the question of whether Madoff should have happened at all. Could his clients, with just a nominal amount of due diligence, have uncovered red flags that would have caused them to walk away?

Many of his investors spent more time researching their next vacation than the man and firm that would impact their standards of living and future financial security.

Why is that? There are four amazing answers that can affect any investor.

First, they wanted to believe the story of Madoff as a financial savant who had developed a sophisticated investment strategy that produced solid, positive returns, even in down markets.

Second, they may have been referred to Madoff by someone they trusted, so they did not think there was any reason to conduct their own due diligence.

Third, they believed the image he created was real.

And fourth, they were too complacent to conduct their own research.

HOW WE "UNCOVERED" BERNIE MADOFF

Our first book, *Who's Watching Your Money?*, was published in 2003. The Paladin Registry website (www. PaladinRegistry.com), which was based on the principles outlined in the book, was launched in April 2004. It was the first online resource that educated investors about financial advisors and provided a registry of vetted, documented financial professionals and firms.

The day after Madoff's arrest, Paladin's advisor research team utilized the internet to vet Bernie Madoff and his firm. We were curious to see what we would find, and it was a way to test the effectiveness of our due diligence process.

It took just forty minutes to complete the research, and the results clearly identified Madoff as a serious risk.

Imagine, forty minutes could have saved eleven thousand investors $50 billion.

Paladin's due diligence on Madoff occurred after his arrest, so we had to act quickly before law enforcement and the regulatory agencies shut down his website and online records at FINRA and the SEC (see below).

In a matter of minutes, using the internet, Paladin was able to identify several red flags that should have warned investors about the legitimacy of Madoff's investment claims and his business model.

FINANCIAL INDUSTRY REGULATORY AUTHORITY (FINRA)

As we will explain in more detail in a later chapter, the FINRA website is the first place you should go when you are researching financial advisors because you can view their record of compliance. In particular, you should look for any client complaints or disciplinary actions on their records. Complaints can be frivolous or serious, but any history of complaints should at least be a cause for concern.

Madoff was registered as a broker-dealer with the National Association of Securities Dealers (NASD), which later became FINRA. Although his Ponzi scheme was conducted through a separate, investment advisory company, he was still subject to FINRA regulations for his broker-dealer activities. His FINRA report did contain several violations involving his trading activities as a broker-dealer for which he was censured three times (twice for the same violation) over a nine-year period with total fines of $45,000. He also received fourteen cautionary letters for technical and/or reporting violations.

While many of these violations appeared to be routine and were not related to his Ponzi scheme, when one person or firm has this many infractions, it is a warning to proceed with caution. From our perspective, any firm that breaks the rules in the past will break the rules in the future. FINRA data supports this conclusion, showing that advisors with one violation are 50 percent more likely to commit another violation at some point in the future.

How do you trust this individual with your assets, in particular, large sums of money that you will depend on for a secure, comfortable retirement?

SECURITIES AND EXCHANGE COMMISSION (SEC)

Madoff provided financial advice for a fee, so Paladin's

next internet stop was the SEC's website to review the firm's Form ADV.

For many years, Madoff represented himself as a money manager, but he did not register with the SEC until 2006. That is a major violation that was overlooked by the regulatory agencies, and it should have been a major red flag for anyone who was familiar with SEC registration requirements for money management firms.

We also discovered some additional red flags for Madoff's firm:

- Madoff's Form ADV was revealing both for what it did and did not disclose. The form should have included information about the principals' backgrounds, but Madoff omitted responses to several of the questions.
- There was also no disclosure of a third party that executed trades for client portfolios. Typically, asset managers have all their trades executed by a major brokerage firm so the trades can be verified by outside auditors. His FINRA registration revealed he had a relationship with an independent securities broker; but, as it turns out, both he and his brother were officers of the company, which was located in the same office as Madoff's investment company.

He later admitted in court he had not traded any securities since the early 1990s.

- There was no mention of an independent custodian that had physical possession of client assets. Registered Investment Advisors (RIAs) are not allowed to have physical contact with client assets, except their fees. That is the role of a custodian, preferably a major brand-name firm—for example: Schwab, Fidelity, Pershing, or TD Ameritrade.

- Madoff's performance reports and track record should have been produced by an independent accounting firm—preferably another name-brand firm. Instead, his fake reports were fabricated by a small CPA firm that operated out of a two-room office located in a suburban strip mall. The CPA who owned the firm was later found to be complicit in perpetrating Madoff's fraudulent activities.

All of this information was available on the internet. Any prudent investor, who had access to this information, would have rejected Madoff's investment scam. Unfortunately, that is not what happened, and the results were devastating.

THE MADOFF WEBSITE

The next stop for Paladin's research team was the Madoff website. You can learn a lot about financial advisors on their websites based on what they do and do not tell you.

Madoff's website was extraordinarily bad. Most of the information you expect to find on an advisor's website was missing. Instead, there was a convoluted description of a derivatives-based "black box" investment strategy. The term "black box" refers to an investment strategy based on an algorithm that is supposed to be so complex that investors cannot possibly understand it. It became an act of faith that the "black box" could produce the results that were claimed by Madoff.

Investors had to believe Madoff was smarter than everyone else for his scam to work.

MADOFF IN THE NEWS

Our last stop was the media. We searched for online news articles about Madoff, using various search terms combined with the name "Madoff," such as "news," "investigations," "complaints," "fraud," and "lawsuits." A few articles popped up that were additional cause for concern.

One article from 2001 caught our eye. It was published in *Barron's* and was titled "Don't Ask, Don't Tell" by Erin Arvedlund. The article questioned Madoff's secretive strategy and how it earned double-digit returns for decades with virtually no negative months. What did Madoff know that thousands of other investment professionals did not know?

Hedge fund managers, who were familiar with Madoff's results, also said his returns could not be replicated using several of their investment models. No one claimed Madoff was cooking the numbers, but there was speculation that he may have been front-running trades through his brokerage firm.

Another article that was published in an industry journal (*MARHedge*) included interviews with more than a dozen investment experts who said they were baffled by the way Madoff was able to generate consistently positive returns regardless of market conditions.

His scam already sounds too good to be true.

While none of the articles alleged fraud, prudent investors should have taken notice and questioned whether investing in something they did not understand was a good idea.

As a result of these articles as well as allegations of fraud made directly to the SEC by an investigator, the

SEC did conduct an investigation of Madoff. However, in 2004 it cleared Madoff of any wrongdoing.

Both FINRA and the SEC faced severe criticism for their failure to uncover Madoff's scam. Both were forced to defend their lack of oversight before Congress, and to this day, neither agency has accepted responsibility or been held accountable for letting Madoff operate his scam for so many years.

IT'S YOUR MONEY!

If you were a Madoff victim, you could place a lot of the blame on the regulatory agencies for failing to protect your financial interests. But what about your responsibility as the owner of the assets? It would have been your decision to invest with Madoff.

It's fairly safe to say that, between new regulations and the strengthening of enforcement standards by both FINRA and the SEC, nothing on the scale of a Bernie Madoff scheme should happen again. However, each year thousands of investors are impacted by smaller scams, and millions more are impacted by bad financial advice.

If you have never been victimized by a scam, you may have the mindset that this can't happen to you. Your advisor is a trustworthy financial expert—maybe even a friend. We hope you are right, but it still pays to use the internet to verify information that is provided to you by advisors.

There are eleven thousand Madoff victims who wished they had done that.

TOP FIVE TAKEAWAYS

- Use the internet to research public data about advisors before you select them.
- Do not let financial advisors control all of the information that you will rely on to make your selection decision.
- Selecting a financial advisor is a business decision that should be based on an objective research process that is not impacted by the advisor's sales skills.
- If it is too good to be true, it is probably not true.
- Do not assume the SEC and FINRA will protect you. A lot of bad advisors have active licenses and registrations.

CHAPTER 2

WHAT YOU MAY NOT KNOW ABOUT FINANCIAL ADVISORS

This chapter is going to be a wake-up call when you read about Wall Street business practices that have the potential to damage your financial interests.

You have seen the headlines and read articles about Wall Street business practices that have damaged millions of investors. What you haven't read is that these practices are a small percentage of a much bigger problem. There are no headlines about less sensational business practices that damage more investors than the schemes and scams you read about.

You may believe these business practices can't impact you, but you would be wrong. Any investor in America, who relies on advisors, can be impacted by bad financial advice and business practices that put the advisor's interests first.

How does the industry get away with it? Regulations are supposed to protect investors. But the agencies that provide the protection are controlled or influenced by Wall Street:

- FINRA is financed by Wall Street firms.
- The SEC is influenced by politicians.
- Wall Street spends millions on lobbyists.
- The lobbyists make sure rules favor Wall Street.
- These agencies have very limited enforcement capabilities.

Investors also make it easy for Wall Street to take advantage of them when they let advisors control how they make their selection decisions.

WHY FINANCIAL ADVISORS?

We write about financial advisors because they are responsible for convincing you to buy Wall Street's products and services. Sure, there are executives who control their firms' business practices, but we are not going to change the way they choose to run their companies.

But we can change the way you select and monitor financial advisors.

BUSINESS PRACTICES

This chapter is focused on industry-wide business practices and red flags that have the potential to damage your financial interests.

You have to be able to recognize the practices and red flags so you can avoid them.

MINIMUM STANDARDS

When you visit a doctor, you assume he is qualified to provide medical advice and services. Your assumption is based on the requirements to enter the medical profession: degrees, internships, residencies, and comprehensive examinations. The same can be said for other types of professionals you depend on for specialized financial advice and services.

The financial service industry has an important role in society. For example, it helps people accumulate and preserve assets for retirement. Its advice and services have a major impact on the financial well-being of millions of people.

However, it is a major mistake to assume that the financial service industry has minimum standards like other professions.

SALES CULTURE

The financial service industry should have minimum standards for education, experience, and certifications, but there are no meaningful standards.

Some companies may have higher standards than an industry that has next to none.

This makes selecting a financial advisor a very risky proposition. There is a big range in quality that varies by firm and professional.

Why are there no meaningful industry standards?

The financial service industry is dominated by a powerful sales culture that puts more emphasis on the production of revenue than it does on the knowledge of its advisors.

Other professionals do not work in industries that are dominated by sales cultures. For example, a doctor puts more emphasis on sound medical advice than how much revenue he can produce from his advice.

We should also add there are thousands of very high-quality advisors who take their profession very seriously. They have college degrees, years of experience, and certifications from accredited organizations.

These are the professionals you are looking for when you select a financial advisor.

CREDENTIALS

There are three primary types of credentials that impact the knowledge of financial advisors: education, experience, and certifications.

There should be minimum requirements for each one, but there are not.

Some advisors misrepresent their credentials to look more knowledgeable than they really are, but more about that later in this book.

EDUCATION REQUIREMENTS

If you are like most investors, you assume financial advisors must have a minimum amount of education to be employed in the industry—just like doctors, lawyers, and CPAs in their professions.

Bad assumption. The financial service industry does not have a minimum education requirement—not even a high school diploma.

There are some excellent advisors who do not have college degrees. These advisors offset their lack of formal education with years of experience, relevant certifications, and other industry-specific learning programs.

EXPERIENCE REQUIREMENTS

Education is one of the quicker ways to acquire knowledge, but it takes years of financial service experience to convert knowledge into competent advice. It is the competent advisors who provide the best financial advice and services.

Like education, the financial service industry does not have a minimum experience requirement—not one day.

A word of caution: Do not equate chronological age with financial service experience. For example, many advisors had careers in other industries before entering financial services. A forty-year-old advisor may have a few months of financial services experience. A thirty-year-old advisor may have years of experience.

Want to know how little importance Wall Street puts on education and experience? The minimum age to be a financial advisor is eighteen.

INDUSTRY CERTIFICATIONS

The easiest way to acquire specialized financial knowledge is a certification program that has minimum requirements, a substantial curriculum, testing, and a continuing education program.

Very high-quality certifications include CFA®, CPA, CFP®, and CIMA. All of them require substantial study and comprehensive testing.

But there is a little-known dark side to this business practice. Advisors may buy credentials, including college degrees and certifications, to look more knowledgeable than they really are.

There are no meaningful industry regulations that prevent this deceptive business practice.

ADVISOR TITLES

When searching for advisors, you should know that titles can be very misleading. In this book, we use the term "financial advisor" or "advisor" in the generic sense because it is the most widely used title in the profession, whether it is accurate or not.

Advisors, in particular salespeople, will use the titles they believe will produce the least amount of resistance when they sell investment and insurance products. For example, an insurance agent may call himself a financial planner to sell more insurance.

Wall Street uses titles to blur the distinctions between sales reps and real financial advisors.

MANDATORY DISCLOSURE REQUIREMENTS

One blatant industry practice is the lack of mandatory disclosure requirements that financial advisors must provide to investors. Wall Street has spent millions of dollars on lobbyists who fight various forms of disclosure that benefit investors.

Why fight disclosure? Disclosure would level the playing field between advisors and investors. In the absence of disclosure, you are more likely to select the financial advisor with the best sales skills, which benefits

Wall Street firms that employ or license hundreds of thousands of skilled sales representatives.

SALES PITCHES

Another business practice worth noting is the use of sales pitches to sell financial advice and services. On a positive note, you could look at a sales pitch as a way to obtain the information you need to make the right selection decision.

There is also the ominous side to sales pitches that far outweighs any perceived benefits. Sales pitches do the following:

- They give advisors control over information you will rely on to make your decision.
- They give advisors control over the process you use to make your selection decision.
- They are verbal so you have no record of what was said to you.

Sales pitches benefit financial advisors and create hidden risks for you.

COMPLIANCE RECORDS

Financial advisors and their firms are in a business

that is based on trust. You have to be able to trust the advice you get from your financial advisor.

Based on this need for trust, you might assume that financial advisors who have a history of investor complaints or disciplinary actions on their compliance records are automatically expelled from the industry. However, that would be a bad assumption.

Many advisors with multiple complaints on their records continue to sell investment products and services.

According to a 2016 study entitled "The Market for Financial Adviser Misconduct" (Source: FINRA), nearly fifty thousand financial advisors engaged in some form of misconduct that produced a disciplinary action, such as a fine, temporary suspension, restitution, or another action.

Only 48 percent of the advisors lost their jobs, and nearly half of those managed to find another job in the industry within twelve months. Only 27 percent of the fifty thousand were no longer in the industry after twelve months.

DON'T ASK, DON'T TELL

A more subtle industry business practice is what advisors choose not to tell you in their sales pitches. They purposely leave out any information that may cause you to reject their sales recommendations.

It is up to you to ask the right questions. If you fail to ask the questions, the advisor is not obligated to provide that information.

They have everything to gain and nothing to lose when they use this business practice.

Some of the information they prefer not to discuss includes the following:

- Their lack or education, experience, or meaningful certifications
- Their records of compliance with industry regulations
- The total amount of expense that is deducted from your accounts
- How they are compensated, how much, by whom, and for what

You are going to have to ask the right questions to obtain "don't tell" information that is withheld by advisors who do not want you to have the information.

RED FLAGS

Some industry business practices produce "red flags" that act as warnings for potential dangers that can impact your financial interests. Most of the red flags are associated with sales tactics that less scrupulous advisors use to gain control of your assets.

Like many warning signs, you may only get one, and there is substantial risk if you choose to ignore it. For example, Bernie Madoff did not use the services of a brand-name custodian for client assets. This was a red flag that was ignored by his victims.

You have to be able to identify red flags to avoid them.

When you experience a red flag, take these steps:

- Conduct additional research to learn more.
- Contact FINRA, the SEC, or a state agency.
- Determine the seriousness of the red flag.
- If it is serious, exclude the advisor from your search.

Some red flags are easy to spot, while others require some thought and research. For example, an advisor uses fake credentials to convince you he is an expert. If you know this, you can avoid selecting the advisor.

Following are some of the most frequent red flags

you will experience when you research, interview, and select financial advisors.

Misrepresentation: Your research shows an advisor is misrepresenting information about his credentials, ethics, business practices, or services.

Omission: Your research shows an advisor is omitting important information about his credentials, ethics, business practices, or services.

Financial Fiduciary: The advisor will not acknowledge in writing that he is a financial fiduciary.

Compliance Record: The advisor has one or more complaints, fines, censures, or suspensions on his compliance record.

Fake Degrees: The advisor has one or more college degrees from nonaccredited schools you have never heard of.

Fake Certifications: The advisor has several initials after his name that mean nothing to you. Upon further scrutiny, you determine the certifications were purchased from a third party.

High Return with Low Risk: This Madoff-type "promise" is a blatant scam. You cannot earn high returns with low risk. You have to take substantial risk to earn high returns.

Fake Track Records: The advisor uses a reference or mutual fund as a track record. The advisor may have selected the mutual fund after the performance occurred.

References: No financial advisor will provide a bad reference. Many references have been coached by advisors to make the right comments.

Expenses: Exclude advisors who are not willing to disclose, in writing, all of the expenses that will be deducted from your accounts.

Compensation: Exclude advisors who will not disclose, in writing, how they are compensated, how much they are compensated, and who compensates them.

Free Advice: Avoid advisors who say they provide free advice and services. "Free" means they are being paid by third parties to sell you their products. The third parties mark up the fees they charge you to recover their marketing expenses.

Free Lunch: Advisors offer to buy lunch to create

competitive advantage for themselves when they sell investment services. You may even feel indebted to the advisor. Go to lunch after you select the advisor.

Performance Reports: Avoid advisors who do not provide performance reports. This could mean they are salespeople. Make performance reports a mandatory service when you select a financial advisor.

Celebrity Endorsements: The SEC issued a warning that the quality of a financial product is not impacted by a celebrity who is paid a substantial fee to promote it.

Verbal Information: Be cautious when all of the information that is provided by the advisor is verbal. You will have no documentation for your records.

INVESTORS MAKE IT EASY

Too many investors make it easy for financial advisors to deceive them. That is because advisors know very few investors will take the time to do the following:

- Research their backgrounds.
- Validate their sales claims.
- Require documentation for key information.

Why is it so easy to deceive investors? Investors let advisors use sales tactics to control the processes they use to make their selection decisions.

We want to transfer control of the selection process back to you where it belongs. The more you know about advisors, the higher the probability is that you will select the best advisor for the right reasons.

TOP FIVE TAKEAWAYS

- There are no minimum standards for education or experience in the financial service industry.
- Measuring financial knowledge is difficult. It is a combination of education, experience, and certifications that require study, testing, and continuing education.
- You have to be able to identify red flags to avoid them.
- Trust what you see, not what you hear, when you evaluate the qualifications of financial advisors.
- Do not assume big firms have higher standards. They are in business, like everyone else, to make money from your assets.

CHAPTER 3

THE INTERNET HAS CHANGED THE GAME

Selecting a financial advisor is a game because you can win or lose.

You win the game if you select a competent, ethical advisor who helps you achieve critical financial goals that include a comfortable retirement and security late in life.

You lose the game if you select a low-quality advisor who sells you expensive, risky, underperforming investment products.

The internet is your key to winning the game.

THAT WAS THEN

Just a few short years ago, there was a good chance financial advisors initiated contact by calling you, sending you an invitation to a free seminar, or joining an organization that you belonged to.

Advisors had to initiate contact to sell you their services and products.

Equally important, advisors controlled virtually all of the information you needed to evaluate their credentials, ethics, business practices, and services. Since most of this information was delivered to you verbally in the form of a sales pitch, it was easy for advisors to use deceptive sales tactics.

Of course, you could have used the internet to research advisors several years ago, but how many investors actually did that? Not many. Most investors accepted being contacted by financial advisors, and they selected the one they liked the best.

The typical investor was making decisions based on the information that was controlled by advisors. They heard what advisors wanted them to hear.

THIS IS NOW

Those days are over. The internet has changed the game—forever. It provides access to a new level of transparency that helps you select the best financial advisor for the right reasons.

When you use the internet to protect your financial interests, advisors are no longer your sole source of information that determines whom you select. All you have to do is know how to use the internet to find, research, contact, and monitor financial advisors.

The internet has leveled the playing field between you and the financial advisors who want to plan your financial future and invest your assets.

The internet does more than just level the playing field. It gives you control over the process you use to select a financial advisor:

- You can determine whom you want to research.
- You can research advisors before you contact them.
- You can maintain your anonymity during the process.
- You can determine whom you contact for interviews.
- You can make objective decisions based on facts.

You already know how easy it is to find what you are looking for on the internet. Next to the internet itself, Google Search may be the greatest technological advancement in the last one hundred years. You can access vast amounts of information that help you make better decisions.

EXPOSING THE WALL STREET SALES CULTURE

It stands to reason that the less you know about planning and investing, the more vulnerable you are to salespeople who claim to be financial experts. Are they real experts, or are they salespeople masquerading as experts?

Your vulnerability increases exponentially when you do not know much about the financial advisors.

As far as Wall Street is concerned, the less you know about advisor credentials, ethics, and business practices, the easier it is to take advantage of your need for financial advice and services. This general lack of knowledge exposes you to a major financial risk—you select a bad advisor for the wrong reasons.

The sales practices of financial advisors expose the ugly underbelly of a culture that dominates Wall Street.

Very few financial firms grow because they deliver superior advice and services. Firms grow because they have superior marketing, advertising, PR, and vast distribution systems comprised of hundreds or thousands of salespeople.

Most investors do not stand a chance against these highly skilled salespeople. Many of them are so good they can convince you they are real financial experts even when it is not true.

The game changed when the internet gave you access to the critical information you need to identify and select real financial experts. However, it is not just access to information. The internet also made it more dangerous for advisors to misrepresent or omit important information when they market their advice and services to you.

Wall Street's iron grip on your advisor selection process is gradually receding. But you are going to have to commit some time to learning more about the ways the internet can help you make the right decisions when you select a financial advisor.

WHO INITIATES CONTACT?

You will not select the best advisor if you limit your search to advisors who contact you.

You have to control whom you talk to. This is one of the biggest impacts of the digital age. Although you may still be solicited by Wall Street salespeople, their ability to contact you is becoming increasingly difficult. Thanks to Caller ID and the National Do Not Call Registry, you are much less likely to be contacted by financial advisors who make hundreds of telemarketing calls per day.

You should not buy investment products over the telephone, and you should not respond to advisors who contact you. Why? There is a 99 percent chance the advisor is a sales representative who is willing to put up with a lot of rejection to get in front of you.

The same goes for junk mail that offers a free lunch at a local steakhouse. This means the advisor is willing to spend serious money just to meet you. Why? Meeting you is the first step in his sales process. Direct mail offers should go in your trash can.

The internet gives you control over the advisors you interview. You only talk to advisors who successfully complete your research process.

One last point: You may be contacted by an advisor who was given your name by someone you trust. It could be a friend, family member, associate, or your CPA. This was one of Bernie Madoff's most successful marketing tactics.

You still have to research the referred advisor's qualifications before you interview him. The referral source may or may not know a good advisor from a bad one. Referral sources can also have conflicts of interest.

INFORMATION IS REAL POWER

We can thank the internet for many remarkable changes in our lives, changes that we already take for granted. It has made us all smarter, more efficient, and more empowered when we make decisions. We have instant access to billions of pages of information and the ability to quickly narrow down our search to the relevant information we actually want to see.

Online access to this information gives us the control we need to select the best financial advisors for the right reasons.

You already know how to use the internet to find and research services and products. This book will show you how to use the internet for the specific purpose of finding, researching, contacting, and selecting the best financial advisors.

ANONYMITY IS POWER

How is this power? You can use the internet to learn a lot about financial advisors, and they don't know you exist. There is no contact until you are ready to interview the advisors you have pre-screened. You control whom you contact.

There is no other way to find and research advisors and retain your anonymity until you are ready to talk to them.

MINIMIZE SUBJECTIVITY

The biggest mistake investors can make is to allow subjectivity to influence their advisor selection decisions.

Intuition is not the right way to select the best financial advisor.

In fact, subjectivity makes it easy for salespeople to prey on investors who make emotion-backed decisions. For example, they use greed and fear to sell particular financial products.

The information on the internet enables you to make objec-

tive selection decisions that are based on facts and not sales pitches.

Sure you can find sales content on financial advisor websites. But you also have access to a lot of other information that is not controlled by the advisors. It is the addition of this information that will help you make the right decision when you select a financial professional or firm.

Any potential subjectivity has to come at the end of your selection process when you choose between two equally qualified finalists. Then, and only then, should you select the one you would most "like" to work with.

MONITORING CURRENT ADVISORS

This book is focused on describing how to use the internet to access public information that will help you select the best financial advisor.

We also included a chapter for those of you who already have current financial advisors and have no intention of replacing them. This later chapter describes several ways you can use the internet to monitor your current advisor.

Why monitor current advisors? You do not want to

be blindsided by an event or advisor problem that has the potential to damage your financial interests. For example, the advisor is censured by a regulatory agency or files for personal bankruptcy.

You want to identify problems as soon as possible so you can minimize their impact on your assets and financial future.

THE IMPACT OF THE INTERNET

The shift in the control of information, from Wall Street salespeople to Main Street investors, is just beginning to impact the financial service industry's business practices.

All industries resist change, but the internet is too powerful to resist. Like it or not, the change is happening and there is nothing Wall Street can do about it—except adapt to some new realities.

Just as the internet impacted other industries, it is beginning to impact the relationships between investors and their financial advisors. It has already ushered in new types of advisors and services, such as robo and virtual advisors.

Amazon used the internet to replace many of the

brick-and-mortar bookstores. Investors are using the internet to change the way they select and retain financial advisors.

And it is not just the millennials who are more comfortable with technology. It is also their parents and grandparents who control trillions of dollars of assets.

All of this control and power is at your fingertips. You just have to know how to use it.

THE NEXT FEW CHAPTERS

The next five chapters in this book describe five steps that will help you select the best financial advisor:

- How to find advisors
- How to research advisors
- How to contact advisors
- How to interview advisors
- How to select the best advisor

TOP 5 TAKEAWAYS

- You have to control the selection process if you want to select the best financial advisor.
- You have to control information to make objective decisions.

- If you want to control the process, you have to be willing to find, research, and contact financial advisors.
- The internet has changed the game by shifting the control of information from Wall Street to Main Street.
- The internet is a powerful tool if you know where to go and what to look for.

CHAPTER 4

HOW TO FIND FINANCIAL ADVISORS

In the past, if you had a financial advisor, chances are you didn't find him. He found you. Just about every investor in America is listed in multiple databases that can be purchased by advisors. The net result was unwanted solicitations by telephone (usually during dinner) and pounds of junk mail that showed up in your mailbox.

Advisors had to initiate contact to sell you investment and insurance products. There is a good chance you did not want the contact, so it was an invasion of your privacy.

Wall Street has a long history of aggressive sales tactics.

There is an even bigger issue. The advisors contacting you were aggressive salespeople. They had to be to put up with massive amounts of rejection to make a sale. We can also say, based on years of experience evaluating their business practices, that this is not the way high-quality financial advisors market their services.

Therein lies your challenge. You have to find higher-quality advisors because very few of them are going to spend time trying to contact you.

Aggressive marketing tactics have not gone away. A high percentage of financial advisors are still skilled salespeople with the ability to charm you into liking them. They know people trust people they like. If you limit your search to financial advisors who contact you, there is an increased risk you will select the wrong advisor.

Why limit your choices to advisors who contact you when it is easy to use the internet to find higher-quality advisors?

USING THE INTERNET TO FIND THE BEST ADVISORS

No doubt you have used the internet to find people

who provide various types of specialized services, such as accountants, attorneys, architects, and so on. You knew what you needed, and you used the internet to find some local experts and conduct your research—let's call it comparison shopping.

This first "how to" chapter describes best practices for using the internet to find high-quality financial advisors. Depending on where you live, there are hundreds or even thousands of financial advisors in your area. And due to the growth of virtual advisors, the universe of quality advisors is ever expanding. With the internet, the location of the advisor is no longer a constraint. In this chapter, you are going to learn how to quickly narrow your search to the ones who meet your selection criteria.

Finding financial advisors, using the internet, is easy.

KEYWORD SEARCHES

Any search engine will get the job done, but we recommend Google because it is responsible for 72 percent of the search traffic.

Step one is to enter the right keywords to refine your search based on the financial expertise or services you are seeking. The two most common sets of keywords are "financial advisor" and "financial planner." These keywords are going to produce pages and pages of results for you.

There is also a large list of secondary keywords such as "wealth manager," "retirement planner," "investment advisor," "certified financial planner," and "money manager." Financial professionals use a variety of titles to describe their roles and services.

INFORMATION OR PROFESSIONALS

There is a big difference between the keywords you use to find information and the keywords you use to find professionals. For example, you might enter "financial planning" to find information about planning and "financial planner" to find professionals who provide planning services.

KEYWORD STRINGS

You can also add keywords to create strings that further refine your search. For example, you enter "CFP Financial Planner." Other frequently used keywords are "RIA," "Fiduciary," "Fee-Only," "CFA," "CIMA," "Retirement Planner," "Estate Planner," and "Tax Planner."

You may also want to use qualitative keywords such as

"Find the Best Financial Advisor." This does not really change the outcome, because Google cannot identify the best advisors. It will match you to advisors who use the word "best" on their websites and in articles they write.

The more keywords you add, the fewer search results you will get, which is what you want. You use keywords to refine searches and exclude financial advisors who don't meet your specific criteria.

To localize your search to a specific city or region, you simply add the city and state to your keyword string as in "Financial Advisors Dallas Texas." That will produce an organic listing of advisors in your area.

It's important to note that the Google My Business search results do not include financial advisors who did not register their business with this service.

There is one concern. Let's say you live in a suburb near a major city. There may be very few high-quality financial advisors in your suburb, but a large number of advisors in the big city. You may want to enter the name of the big city in the search engine so you have more choices.

KEYWORDS FOR SPECIALISTS

Most advisors work with individual investors or institutional investors (pension, endowment, foundation). Some advisors work with both.

At the other end of the spectrum are the advisors who specialize in particular niches. If you are seeking a specialist, you may want to add keywords that apply to you: "millennials," "retirees," "pre-retirees," "business owners," "divorcees," or "doctors." For example, if you are looking for advisors who work in the medical community, your keyword string might look like this: "Financial Advisors for Doctors in Dallas Texas".

SEARCH RESULTS

The results of your search to find financial advisors are going to be served to you on hundreds of pages.

When you use Google to find advisors, its current format is to display the following:

- Three or four paid advertisers at the top of the page
- Three local firms under Google My Business
- Ten organic results in the middle of the page
- Three paid advertisers at the bottom of the page

There are a lot of choices on page one, which is why 91.8 percent of users do not scroll to page two. There are a lot of choices on page one, but they may not be your best choices.

Most of the organic search results will display financial firms or professionals in your area. However, some of the top organic listings will be for .orgs (nonprofits), .edus (educational organizations), and content that contains the keywords you input into the Google search function.

You can find high-quality advisors by reading their content and clicking on links that take you to their websites.

You should scan a minimum of two to three pages of Google search results so you have more choices. The best advisors may not be able to afford page one visibility.

PAID ADVERTISERS

All financial advisors want to be represented on page one of Google for keywords that impact their businesses. Consequently, the competition is fierce for page-one placement because Google algorithms control organic rankings and there are a limited number of advertising opportunities.

As you might imagine, advertising space is dominated by companies with bigger marketing budgets. Many of the best advisors do not have big marketing budgets.

Why advertise? Higher organic rankings can take

advisors months, years, or may never be achieved. If they are willing to pay Google enough money, like any other advertising resource, they can appear on page one tomorrow.

This is good for Google because it makes billions of dollars from paid advertising. It is good for the paid advertisers because they get instant visibility on page one. But it may be bad for you when you are seeking the best financial advisors.

There is no relationship between the size of a firm's advertising budget and the quality of the advisors who work for the firm. A high budget just means the company can afford to pay Google and the other search engines for the ad space.

The ads are based on "pay-for-click," which means every time you click on a financial advisor's ad, the advertiser owes Google money. It doesn't matter if you respond to the ad; you just have to click on it to produce revenue for Google and expense for the advertiser.

In general, you will not find boutique firms advertising on Google's page one or on pages that are based on the most popular keywords, such as "financial advisor" or "financial planner." More likely, you will find smaller firms advertising on longer keyword strings such as "Certified Divorce Financial Planner Dallas."

NETWORKS, DIRECTORIES, ASSOCIATIONS

You can enter keywords in search engines to find financial advisors, or you can visit the websites of organizations that sponsor networks, directories, and associations of financial professionals.

You can save a few steps in your search process by using these sources to find financial advisors. In general, the sites provide access to advisors who meet their membership requirements. They also provide a search function by location or other filters that can help you find the professionals you are seeking.

DISCLOSURE

A coauthor of this book founded the Paladin Registry, one of the networks described in this chapter. He is also the author of Who's Watching Your Money? The 17 Paladin Principles for Selecting a Financial Advisor.

The service providers in this chapter are not listed in any particular order.

There may be other websites that provide similar services.

Some networks, directories, and associations vet the advisors who are listed on their websites. Some do little or no vetting. They list anyone who is willing to pay their service fees.

The main motive of some of the organizations that publish directories is to drive traffic to their websites. The traffic enables them to sell advertising for space that is adjacent to their directories.

All organizations that are described in this book are active as of the publication date. We cannot guarantee they will continue to sponsor networks, directories, and associations in the future.

NETWORKS

In general, advisors pay monthly or annual fees to be part of a national network of financial advisors. Networks deliver a wide range of services to advisors including referrals to investors who use the networks to find financial advisors. The value in using networks for your search is that some of them do part of the vetting for you.

Advisors pay various types of service fees for network services.

DIRECTORIES

There are different types of directories. Some are aggregators of data from other sources, such as FINRA and the SEC. They restructure the data to make it more user-friendly. They provide filters that help you sort by criteria that are important to you.

Other directories require financial advisors to submit data by completing a questionnaire. The information in the questionnaire may or may not be vetted by the sponsor of the directory.

Advisors pay various types of service and/or advertising fees to be listed in directories.

ASSOCIATIONS

Associations are organizations that allow advisors who meet their criteria to become members. Some of the associations are nonprofits. To remain in good standing with the organization, members must continuously meet its education and ethics requirements.

Advisors usually pay monthly or annual fees to be members of the associations.

PALADIN REGISTRY
(www.paladinregistry.com)

Paladin Registry reviews and documents financial advisor credentials, ethics, business practices, and services. To be profiled in the registry, financial advisors must be a Registered Investment Advisor (RIA) or Investment Advisor Representative (IAR) and an acknowledged fiduciary.

Paladin also conducts research on financial advisors, reviewing public data from FINRA, the SEC, state securities commissioners, advisor websites, and Google name searches.

Investors have the option of using Paladin's match system or directory to select the advisors they want to interview.

Advisors pay Paladin a subscription fee to participate in this program.

BETTER BUSINESS BUREAU
(www.BBB.org)

The Better Business Bureau (BBB) is one of the most recognized names in America. For more than one hundred years it has been helping consumers make better decisions and avoid low-quality companies and people who take advantage of the public.

The BBB publishes a directory of accredited and non-accredited financial advisors that includes profiles that document key information that describes their qualifications.

You should always check the BBB website before you select a financial advisor.

To find a financial advisor, go to www.BBB.org. In the FIND box, type in "Financial Advisor." In the NEAR box, type in the city and state, and then click on SEARCH. You will be presented with a list of financial advisors who have BBB profiles. You can narrow your search by expanding the filters for minimum BBB ratings, BBB accreditation, and category.

NATIONAL ASSOCIATION OF PERSONAL FINANCIAL ADVISORS
(www.napfa.org)

The National Association of Personal Financial Advisors (NAPFA) has more than 2,500 members consisting of fee-only financial advisors and planners. Membership requirements include CFP certification, a bachelor's degree, submission of a Form ADV Part 2, and completion of sixty hours of NAPFA continuing education every two years.

You can search for advisors by name or location and review their profile page, which details the advisor's practice.

FINANCIAL PLANNING ASSOCIATION
(www.plannersearch.org)

The Financial Planning Association (FPA) is a membership organization for CFP® professionals. Members must be in good standing with the CFP Board of Standards and offer financial planning as one of their services.

The site enables investors to search for advisors by name or location. The listing includes a biography and a list of services provided by the advisor.

CFA INSTITUTE
(www.cfainstitute.org)

The CFA Institute has a worldwide membership of more than 135,000 financial and investment professionals who have completed its rigorous program of study and passed all three levels of examinations. Members must have a bachelor's degree and at least forty-eight months of professional work experience.

Use the Member Directory to find a CFA or verify their membership.

WISERADVISOR
(www.wiseradvisor.com)

WiserAdvisor is one of the oldest and largest independent networks of pre-screened financial advisors. To be listed with WiserAdvisor, advisors must pass a three-step qualification process that includes the completion and verification of an extensive profile outlining their services, qualifications, credentials, and educational background.

You can submit your requirements, and WiserAdvisor will match you to local advisors who meet your requirements.

Advisors pay WiserAdvisor a lead-generation fee for this service.

XY PLANNING NETWORK
(www.xyplanningnetwork.com)

XY Planning Network is a leading organization of fee-only financial advisors who specialize in helping Gen X and Gen Y investors. All members are sworn fiduciaries and must offer a flat (and affordable) monthly fee for their services. Advisors must hold a CFP certification and offer comprehensive financial planning services.

Investors can search by location, age, gender, profession, and interest.

GARRETT PLANNING NETWORK
(www.garrettplanningnetwork.com)

The Garrett Planning Network is a referral network of fee-only financial advisors targeting the middle-income market. Members must be fee-only and adhere to a fiduciary oath. Also, they must be a CFP or a CPA with a Personal Financial Specialist (PFS) designation or obtain either designation within five years of initial RIA registration.

The site is searchable by keyword or location.

GUIDEVINE
(www.guidevine.com)

GuideVine offers both an advisor directory and an advisor match service. Advisors must meet certain minimum requirements to be listed, including years of experience, number of clients, and clean compliance record, and they must be acknowledged fiduciaries.

You can search by geographic region and use filters to narrow down your choices; or you can answer a few questions and have GuideVine connect you to advisors who meet your requirements.

GuideVine allows advisors to post introductory videos that can provide you with another perspective.

This organization charges advisors a fixed fee to participate in this program.

BRIGHTSCOPE
(www.brightscope.com)

BrightScope accesses the FINRA database for its directory listings. It is a more user-friendly version of the FINRA/BrokerCheck database. BrightScope also provides filters you can use to refine your search parameters.

CREDIO
(www.financial-advisors.credio.com)

Credio uses data aggregation technology to download FINRA and SEC information for its directory. You can use a number of filters to narrow your search, including types of compensation, designations, types of services, and registered titles.

ASK A FRIEND

Many higher-quality advisors work on referrals from current clients or other professionals, so you may want to ask people you know and trust for referrals.

You may believe there is no need to research advisors who are recommended by people you trust; however, there is substantial risk when you have no idea what the referral source's selection criteria might be in relation to your own.

Referrals do not eliminate the need for research; they are just an easy way to find advisors.

FIND AN ADVISOR

We recommend you research the network, directory, and association websites to learn more about them before you use their services.

You are bound to find a number of advisors who initially meet some of your criteria. Your next step is to apply the research process outlined in the next chapter to reduce your choices to the advisors you actually want to interview.

TOP FIVE TAKEAWAYS

- The internet gives you control over the advisors you interview and select.
- Finding advisors, using the internet, is fast, easy, and free.
- You should maintain your anonymity the entire time you use the internet to find advisors, until you are ready to initiate contact.
- Advertising on search engines has nothing to do with the quality of financial firms or advisors.
- Do not assume that all directories, networks, and associations have meaningful minimum requirements or vetting.

CHAPTER 5

HOW TO RESEARCH FINANCIAL ADVISORS

You already know, when it comes to your financial future, that selecting the right professional is the most important decision you will make. The right choice will produce more assets for your retirement years and increase your financial security late in life when you need it the most.

What is more important than the financial consequences of this choice?

Researching advisors is the step in your process that determines who you interview. The interview determines which professional you select to be your advisor.

YOUR OBJECTIVITY

Too many investors rely on their intuition when they select financial advisors. What they fail to realize is intuition/emotions/feelings are easy to manipulate by advisors with superior sales skills.

An intuitive selection process can cause you to select the advisor with the best personality and sales skills.

It is very risky to select advisors based on feelings. Your selection process should be based on factual information and objectivity.

Consider how you buy a car. You conduct your research on the internet to determine which cars may interest you. Then you visit multiple dealerships to test-drive the cars. Then you select the car you liked the best based on your needs and budget.

Online research determined which cars you test-drove. Online research determines which advisors you interview.

You have to control the process to make sure you get the information you need to make the right decision.

A PROCESS OF EXCLUSION

The TV show *Survivor* has a few parallels to your process for selecting a financial advisor.

At the beginning of the show, twenty people who don't know each other are dropped in a remote location. At the end of thirty-nine days there is one winner who receives $1 million. The show is based on reducing twenty initial contestants to the one who wins the money.

You also use a process of exclusion when you select a financial advisor. For example, you use the internet to find and research several advisors. Next, you exclude some of the advisors you find for a variety of reasons, and you interview who is left. Ultimately, you select one winner who will be responsible for helping you plan your financial future and invest your assets.

WHY USE EXCLUSION?

Exclusion is an important part of your process because you can start with a bigger number of advisors and reduce it down to one (the winner).

There are one hundred reasons why you may exclude advisors from your search. Some of the more frequent ones are as follows:

- The advisor does not provide the right combination of services.
- The advisor lacks experience.
- The advisor is paid with commissions.
- The advisor charges more than other advisors.
- The advisor does not have the right certifications.
- The advisor lacks communication skills.
- The advisor does not have a succession plan.

RESEARCHING ADVISORS

The internet gives you access to vast amounts of information about financial advisors, but you do not want to spend hours seeking and reviewing information.

You need an efficient way to research an advisor in a matter of minutes.

In this chapter, you will learn where to go on the internet to find the information you need to research financial advisors. The information you uncover will help you identify weaker advisors so you can exclude them from your selection process.

More importantly, the research will help you identify advisors with the best qualifications so you can include them in the next step of your selection process—whom you will contact for the interview.

Utilizing our years of experience vetting thousands of financial advisors, we have mapped out a research process that is easy to follow and use.

For example, we list a number of independent sources along with their website addresses. We show you how to refine your searches for the quickest access to the information you need. We explain what information you are looking for and why it's important.

As you proceed through the sources, you gradually build a picture of the advisor's credentials, ethics, and business practices. This is the information you need to determine who makes it to the next step in your selection process.

DISCLAIMER

The information in this chapter and other chapters describes services and functionality that existed when this book was published. Some services may cease to exist. Some services may change their business practices or operations.

REGULATORY WEBSITES FOR DISCIPLINARY ACTIONS

We start with the regulatory websites because their findings will help you determine the trustworthiness of financial advisors. Why spend time researching advisors who have multiple complaints on their compliance records?

Never select a financial advisor without reviewing his compliance record.

When you find a complaint, you should read the description and the resolution. What if the advisor was absolved of any wrongdoing? Some compliance experts believe 80 percent of all complaints are frivolous.

Why so high? Investors file complaints when they lose money in the stock market. In most cases, these complaints are "denied" in arbitrations that are conducted by the regulatory agencies.

FINRA
(www.finra.org)

FINRA (Financial Industry Regulatory Authority) is a self-regulatory organization that is financed by Wall Street. You would be correct if you concluded that Wall Street regulates itself.

This may mean that FINRA is not as investor-friendly as it should be, but it is your best source for viewing the compliance records of the firms (3,800) and professionals (634,000) who sell investment products for commission.

FINRA was authorized by Congress to protect America's investors by making sure the broker-dealer industry operates fairly and honestly.

BROKERCHECK
(www.brokercheck.finra.org)

BrokerCheck is a FINRA service that enables you to review the compliance records of broker-dealer firms and their registered representatives.

- It maintains records for firms and professionals who hold active securities licenses.
- It retains records for two years for firms and professionals who drop their licenses.
- It maintains records in perpetuity for firms and professionals who have complaints on their records.

You can access BrokerCheck data by entering CRD (Central Registry Depository) numbers or the full names of advisors. CRD numbers are your best choice because they are unique identifiers, but you may not be able to obtain them until after you contact the advisors.

Common advisor names can make your search more difficult. If you only have the name, enter the city where the advisor works to narrow your search.

Disciplinary actions can be more serious, especially if they result in a fine, censure, or suspension. In general, disciplinary actions resulting from ethical misconduct should be grounds for excluding an advisor from your search.

You will also find additional information in BrokerCheck that you can use to validate some of the advisor's claims—for example, years of experience, employment history, and licensing.

SEC
(www.SEC.gov)

Whereas FINRA regulates broker-dealers, the SEC (Securities and Exchange Commission) is a government agency that is tasked with regulating and overseeing Registered Investment Advisors (RIAs) with more than $100 million in assets under management. States regulate RIAs who invest less than $100 million.

When financial advisory firms register with the SEC, they must complete a Form ADV that is as close as you will get to full disclosure for their businesses. Disclosures on Form ADV include ownership, business practices, disciplinary history, financial information, investment processes, and other pertinent information that must be updated annually.

ADVs are a treasure trove of information that you can use to learn what you need to know about firms and their advisors. The amount of information can be overwhelming, but the document is a very useful research tool.

Form ADV has two parts: Part 1 provides the essential data about a firm, including the number of clients, owners and advisors, state registrations, disciplinary information, and so on. Part 2 is more of a narrative that describes the education and backgrounds of advisors, the types of services offered, fees, compensation arrangements, and their methods for selecting investments for their clients.

ADV PART I

Part 1 is mainly yes-and-no and fill-in-the-blank responses to a checklist of questions. The easiest way to view the information in Part 1 is to use the "View Form ADV by Section" option. This enables you to find the information that matters most to you, including the following:

- Information About the Advisor's Business: number of employees, number and types of clients, compensation arrangements, assets under management, and types of advisory activities
- Disclosure Information: lists past charges, convictions, and suspensions
- Disclosure Questions: answers specific questions about disclosure information and potential conflicts of interest

ADV PART 2

ADV Part 2 is referred to as the Firm Brochure, which provides important information that is easier for you to read and understand.

Part 2A contains a lot of information in a narrative form, which takes a fair amount of time to read. The most important information is found in the following six items:

- Fees and compensation
- Types of clients they serve
- Methods of analysis, investment strategies, risk of loss
- Disciplinary information
- Client referrals and other compensation
- Custody of client assets

Part 2B contains resumes for the firm's professionals that include the following information:

- Educational and business experience
- Disciplinary information
- Other business activities
- Compensation
- How the advisor is supervised

HOW TO ACCESS FORM ADV

You have online access to the form on the SEC's Investment Adviser Public Disclosure (IAPD) website at www.adviserinfo.sec.gov. IAPD is a public data repository for RIA firms and their Investment Advisor Representatives (IARs). You can search for information about professionals or firms.

Accessing the Form ADV is easy. All you need to do is enter the firm's name and click on the search button. Then click on the firm's name to access the report. To view its Form ADV, click on "Get Details." You will be able to view both ADV Part 1 and ADV Part 2. They are presented in PDF format so you can print the report for your records.

STATE SECURITIES COMMISSIONERS

Smaller RIAs with assets under $100 million are required to register with their state securities commissioners. You can find out how to contact your state's commissioner by going to the NASAA (North American Securities Administrators Association) website: www.NASAA.org. Click on the "Contact Your Regulator" navigation tab on the far left to find a list of state regulators with their contact information, or you can click on the name of your state to be taken to the website of the regulatory agency.

A high percentage of the advisor information that is maintained by states may not be available online. Contact your state's securities commissioner to find out how to access advisor information.

STATE INSURANCE COMMISSIONER

Most financial advisors provide planning and investment services. A significant percentage of these professionals also have licenses that permit them to sell several types of insurance products, such as annuities, life, disability, health, and long-term care insurance. A very small percentage are licensed to sell casualty insurance products.

The state that issued the license will have a record of

the advisor's licensing and compliance record. This data will vary by state.

Some of the state websites include an agent search application, enabling you to search by name. Go to your state's insurance department or commission to obtain the information you are seeking.

You can also go to the National Association of Insurance Commissioners (NAIC) website at www.naic.org and use their directory to find your state's insurance commissioner.

A high percentage of the advisor information that is maintained by states may not be available online. Contact your state's insurance commissioner to find out how to access advisor information.

FINANCIAL ADVISOR WEBSITES

Just about every financial advisory firm in America has a website. It may be their own website, or advisors may have a biographical page on an employer's website. Some financial advisors, in particular more junior advisors, may not be represented on their firms' websites.

For most advisors, a website can be a powerful marketing tool that acts as their virtual office on the internet. They use several strategies to produce traffic for their websites, and the role of the sites is to convert traffic into leads for their services.

In many respects, financial advisor websites act like online sales brochures (e.g., Who We Are, What We do, Who We Serve, and Contact Us), which can also mean that most of the content on the site is more or less promotional.

These sites may have limited value for investors who want to learn more about advisors before they contact them.

The content on advisor websites is a blend of what advisors do and do not want to tell you.

Higher-quality advisors use their websites to practice transparency. They can afford to be transparent because they have nothing to hide. You will begin to recognize who is transparent and who is not after visiting a few advisor websites.

Following are examples of the types of information you can find on these websites:

- They provide several wealth management services.
  - Does one professional provide several services?
  - Is there a team or firm of professionals?
  - Is there a biography for each professional?
- They say they are financial experts.
  - Look for information that documents education, experience, and certifications.
- They say they are trustworthy.
  - Look for links to FINRA BrokerCheck.
  - Look for a reference to a financial fiduciary.
  - Are they registered? (RIA or IAR)
- They say their business practices are investor-friendly.
  - How are they compensated?
  - Do they disclose all expenses?
  - How do they communicate?
  - Do they provide performance reports?
- What types of clients do they serve?
  - Millennials, pre-retirees, retirees
  - Executives, professionals, business owners
  - High net worth, ultra-high net worth
  - Institutions (pension, endowment, foundation)
  - Most importantly, do they work with clients like you?
- What types of services do they provide?
  - Planning (financial, retirement, estate, college, charitable)
  - Investment (advisory, portfolio management)

- ° Insurance (life, annuity, long-term care)
- ° Tax (planning, preparation)
- ° Legal (wills, trusts, probate)

Advisors who practice full transparency are inherently more trustworthy than advisors who withhold information from potential clients.

Be sure to view the information at the bottom of the home page. It will tell you who the advisor or firm is affiliated with. For example, you might see: *"Securities offered through XYZ Financial, Member FINRA/SIPC."* This tells you the advisory firm is licensed with a broker-dealer, which also means they sell investment products for commissions. If the advisor is an RIA, you will typically see: *"XYZ Financial, a Registered Investment Advisor."* Many RIAs include a link to their Form ADV.

If you want to obtain additional information about an advisory firm, read their online Terms of Service and Privacy Policy documents.

CHECK CREDENTIALS

You want a financial expert who has specialized knowledge and services that can help you achieve your financial goals.

How do advisors prove they are real experts? Verbal information in a sales pitch does not count.

A frequently used tactic is to display several letters (degrees, certifications) after their names that are supposed to represent their sources of expertise. As you read in a previous chapter, the letters after their names may or may not mean they are real financial experts.

Our research showed advisors are using more than 250 certifications and designations and that approximately 35 percent are bogus—that is, the certification had no meaningful prerequisites, curriculums, testing, or continuing education. Or, in some cases, the sponsors of the certifications have gone out of business, but advisors have continued to use their designations.

CHECK THE SOURCE

One way to verify an advisor's credentials is to use the internet to go to the website of the organization that sponsors the certification. Are they still in business? Do they have investor content on their website? What can you learn about the credential on the website? Do they have a directory of professionals who have earned the credential?

The internet makes this process easy. Simply Google

the name of the designation or the letters to bring up the website. Legitimate credentials have informative websites. For example, when you enter "Certified Financial Planner" (CFP) in the search box, the top search result will be the CFP Board of Standards. You can learn more about the credential and use its "Verify Member" function to determine if the advisor you are researching actually holds this credential.

If you cannot find the credential on the internet, there is a good chance it is not real.

CHECK WITH YOUR STATE

Some states are more vigilant than others when they track the designations that advisors use to convince their residents that they are financial experts. You should check with your state's regulatory agencies to determine if they produce reports that document the quality of advisors' credentials.

USE A CREDENTIAL-CHECKING TOOL

Paladin Research & Registry provides a free, no-registration-required service that makes it fast and easy to check the quality of an advisor's credentials.

Go to www.PaladinRegistry.com and click on "Investor Tools / Check a Credential" to access a database of more than 250 certifications and designations that are used by financial advisors.

There is a description for each certification and a quality rating that is based on an algorithm that was developed by Paladin researchers.

A 0-star quality rating is assigned for certifications produced by organizations that no longer exist. Certifications issued by stellar organizations that require substantial study, testing, and continuing education are awarded a 5-star quality rating.

FINRA WEBSITE

The FINRA website also maintains a directory of certifications and designations. It is not as thorough as Paladin's, but it has an alphabetized lookup, and you can click on the credential to learn more about it. The site also enables you to choose multiple credentials to do side-by-side comparisons.

Go to www.finra.org/investors/professional-designations, or you can Google "FINRA professional designations" to find the directory.

BETTER BUSINESS BUREAU

The Better Business Bureau (BBB) is one of the most recognized brands in America. It has provided services to consumers for more than one hundred years. It has always been a go-to resource for researching the quality of businesses and professionals, and it should be a part of your research process.

Utilizing information obtained from public data sources as well as the businesses themselves, BBB rates businesses based on how they interact with their customers, assigning a quality rating from A+ (highest) to F (lowest).

The rating elements include a business's complaint history, response record, time in business, transparency of business practices, licensing and government actions, and truth in advertising. Although BBB ratings are not a guarantee of a business's reliability or performance, the information it gathers to develop business profiles can be helpful in evaluating the quality of financial firms and professionals.

To look up an advisor's BBB profile, enter the advisor's name followed by "BBB" in Google Search. You may have to add the advisor's city if multiple names come up.

The search results will bring up the names of BBB

accredited advisors in your area. Make sure you view the individual profile for the business. If the advisor you're searching for does not appear in the search results, it means BBB has not obtained sufficient information to assign a rating.

GOOGLE NAME SEARCH

In the previous chapter, we described how to use search engines to find financial advisors. The next step is to use the search engines to research firms and advisors.

You are looking for any information that may validate or invalidate the sales claims of financial advisors or other information that would cause you to include or exclude advisors from the next step in your selection process.

This may be information that appears in a regulatory database, or it may not. For example, you might find a negative article written about a financial advisor in your local newspaper. Conversely, you might find that the advisor donates time and money to an important local charity. The information can be positive or negative.

Your internet research should be conducted on the advisor and the advisor's firm. If the firm is privately held, you may want to research the names of the owners of the firm.

To get started, simply enter the advisor's name in the search box. If the advisor has a common name, you can narrow your search by adding the city where he works: "John Smith Dallas Texas" or "John Smith Financial Advisor Dallas Texas."

Your search will bring up all the references to this advisor, including his firm's website and the advisor's social media sites. If you want to zero in on news-related items, you can add the word "news" to your keyword string, and this will bring up news articles that mention the advisor's name.

Because you are looking for negative information that would cause you to exclude the advisor from your search, you should also add keywords such as "lawsuit," "bankruptcy," "foreclosure," "liens," "fine," "felony," "arrest," and similar words that are associated with behaviors or events that create risk for you.

You can also look for positive information by inputting keywords for connections to churches, social groups, schools, and nonprofits that may be supported by the advisor.

What if there is no information—positive or negative? You could think no news is good news, but that is a little risky at this point. Remember:

- High-quality advisors tend to be active in their communities.
- They have done something that is newsworthy.
- They contribute articles to blog sites.
- They have been recognized by various organizations.

SOCIAL MEDIA SITES

Disclaimer: We do not recommend using personal social media accounts for any type of profiling based on race, sex, religion, age, or political affiliations. You can use business social media accounts to learn more about advisors or firms before you select them.

You can learn a lot about financial advisors by visiting their firms' social media pages. Facebook, LinkedIn, Instagram, and Twitter are among the more widely used social media platforms, and they can provide information about the advisor's knowledge and credibility.

All financial advisors do not use social media for their businesses. In fact, those who work for broker-dealers may be limited by compliance rules in regard to how they can use social sites.

Advisors who include social media in their digital marketing strategies are usually very cautious about how they use the various sites and avoid posting information that could damage their reputation.

RIAs are more likely to use social media as part of a web marketing strategy because they have more freedom to use the internet to grow their businesses.

The number of social media sites continues to grow, but we recommend you concentrate on the more popular sites, which are more likely to be used by financial advisors.

The easiest way to find an advisor's social media sites is to Google his name. The sites should show up on page one of the search results.

FACEBOOK

Facebook is a social site used primarily by individuals to engage with their friends and family. However, it is also used by some advisors to interact with their ideal types of clients. Advisors may use Facebook for social engagement, but they may also have a separate professional page dedicated to their businesses.

By entering the firm's name in the search box, any page associated with the advisor will come up in the search results. By viewing his professional page, you can see how he engages with his community.

LINKEDIN

LinkedIn is primarily a professional networking site. Individuals use LinkedIn to interact with peers and other members of their industry. They also use it to network with the rest of the LinkedIn community. Advisors who know how to use LinkedIn will post articles and information to demonstrate their value as thought leaders.

YOUTUBE

An increasing number of advisors are using YouTube to post videos as a way to promote their businesses. The videos are typically about financial topics that can help you evaluate the advisor's knowledge and communication skills.

ITUNES

You can check iTunes to see if an advisor has posted any podcasts. Similar to videos, podcasts are used to present financial information and tips.

THE FAKE ADVISOR

What if your research does not turn up any information about particular advisors on the internet? This should be grounds for automatic exclusion. You do not have to know why there is no information. All you have to know is the lack of information creates a hidden risk, which you can avoid by excluding these advisors from your selection process.

It is possible that you are researching a scam artist who does not have the required licensing and registration to be marketing financial advice and services for compensation.

In extreme cases, criminals and others pose as financial advisors to gain control of your assets. They may even steal the identity of legitimate advisors. This is one of the more important reasons why you should cross-check the information you find on multiple websites.

You may even want to match photos on the internet to the advisors you are interviewing.

TOP FIVE TAKEAWAYS

- Intuition is the wrong way to select a financial advisor.
- Factual information and validation is the right way to select a financial advisor.

- Excluding advisors helps you narrow your search, but you should exclude them for the right reasons.
- Always start your research with the regulatory agencies. Why waste time researching unethical advisors?
- The internet is your best way to research advisors before you contact them.

CHAPTER 6

HOW TO CONTACT FINANCIAL ADVISORS

You have completed your research and identified three or four advisors you would like to interview. The interview is the last step before you make your selection decision, but there is an interim step. You have to initiate contact with advisors to schedule their interviews.

When you initiate contact, you determine which advisors will be interviewed.

We wrote this chapter because we know initiating contact can be a major concern to some investors.

Yes, Wall Street has a bad reputation for aggressive sales tactics, but that usually occurs when its salespeople control the process. In this case, you control the process and not Wall Street.

Your concerns are understandable, but keep in mind that you only contact financial advisors who made it through your research process. You already know a lot about them, and you should only be contacting high-quality financial professionals and firms.

Your opportunity to control the process should outweigh any concerns you might have about initiating contact.

It's your choice. You can interview advisors who contact you, or you can limit your contacts to advisors who made it through your objective research process.

The advisors you research and contact are your safer choices.

METHOD OF CONTACT

We want to take the guesswork out of initiating contact with financial advisors.

Most investors are reluctant to just pick up the telephone and call financial advisors. They have had too many bad experiences with telemarketers. That leaves two other methods of contact:

- Send the advisors an introductory email asking them to contact you.
- Visit the advisors' websites and initiate contact using the "Contact Us" function.

EMAIL CONTACT

Email is the more convenient way to initiate contact because you retain some of your anonymity. The advisor has your name and email address, but you can still exclude your telephone number if you are concerned about telephone solicitations.

By initiating contact with an email, you also have an opportunity to see how the advisor responds to you. Is the response timely? Does the advisor respond or a subordinate? Did you receive an automated email response?

TELEPHONE CONTACT

Your initial contact may be by email, but we still recommend talking to the advisor before you schedule the interview. This initial contact helps you form a first impression of the advisor's communication skills and approach to prospective clients.

How the advisor communicates on the phone can be very important input. Did he act interested? Did he ask good questions about your current situation and goals? Is he willing to meet at a location that is more convenient for you?

Keep in mind that the advisor does not know you. High-quality professionals are as interested in screening you as you are in screening them.

This initial contact is the beginning of a process that builds trust that is an essential building block for developing a positive relationship with a financial advisor.

WEBSITE CONTACT

Most financial advisors provide contact options on their website. When you click on the "Contact" link, navigation tab, or a "Call to Action" button, you will be taken to a landing page that provides the advisor's contact data and asks for your contact information.

In some cases, you will be asked to provide your name, location, email address, telephone number, and the reason for the contact. Some information is required, and some may be optional.

Internet-savvy advisors are aware of your concerns

about aggressive sales tactics. In this case, they may only ask for your first name and your email address. They will obtain more information when you schedule the interview.

You should provide all of the information that is necessary to initiate contact with the advisor.

PRIVACY POLICY

You may be concerned about how the advisor will protect your contact information. If that is the case, make sure you read the advisor's Privacy Policy. It should explain what the advisor can and cannot do with your contact information. For example, it should state that the advisor will not sell your contact information to third parties.

Your contact data should be for the advisor's exclusive use. The only people who see your information are the advisor and his staff.

Do not initiate contact with advisors if you have any concerns about their policies for protecting your contact data.

HIGH-PRESSURE SALES TACTICS

If you experience high-pressure sales tactics when you contact advisors, you should automatically exclude them from any further consideration in your selection process.

This is one of the ways you exercise control over the process.

High pressure tactics could include the following:

- Aggressive sales tactics during the contact phase
- An obnoxious personality on the telephone
- Asking for information before you are ready to provide it
- Spam emails
- Unwanted telemarketing calls

You may also be uncomfortable with the advisor's personality. Although this is a subjective criterion, you should not ignore your initial impression. If this happens, immediately unsubscribe from future emails, and add the advisor's telephone number to the Do Not Call Registry.

PURPOSE OF THE TELEPHONE CALL

You should have a clear purpose for your call or email. Are you simply scheduling an interview, gathering more information about the advisor, or both?

Your primary goal is to schedule an interview, but you may have a few questions that were not answered in your research phase:

- Do you work with clients who have $100,000 to invest?
- Do you work with individual investors?
- Do you provide planning and investment services?
- Do you have current clients in my area?

FIRST IMPRESSIONS

From the first contact, you should be very aware of your first impressions when you interact with the advisors and their staffs for the first time.

For example, this is an opportunity to form an impression about the quality of the advisors' communications. This is a critical element in your relationship with advisors when they describe their planning and investment processes. Do they use a lot of investment jargon or provide information that you understand?

You should be initiating contact with multiple advisors so that you have choices. This is also your opportunity to start comparing advisors to each other.

In fact, at this point, you may want to start grading them for criteria that are important to you. Communication skills and professionalism should be near the top of your list.

If the advisor does not measure up, compared to the other professionals you are talking to, save yourself some time and tell him you will call back if you are still interested.

Be extra cautious if you find yourself liking an advisor before you know much about him. You want to select the best advisor for the right reasons.

FREE CONSULTATION

Some advisors refer to the first meeting with a prospective client as a free, no-obligation consultation.

This is not a consultation.

You are scheduling an interview for the purpose of gathering additional information to determine whom you will select to be your financial advisor.

The initial consultation occurs after you have made your selection decision. And then it only applies to the advisor you selected.

You may be asked to bring financial documents or

complete a detailed questionnaire prior to the meeting. It is your choice whether or not you do so.

If you're not comfortable providing that information yet, you could remind the advisor that you are still in the process of making your selection decision and that you will provide the information when you make your choice.

On the other hand, providing your advisor candidates with some background information on your finances and goals would allow them to better prepare for the meeting, so they can ask pertinent questions and discuss more specifically how they can help you.

The free consultation is a sales tactic that some advisors use to control the interview.

This tactic should make you uncomfortable.

YOUR INTERESTS COME FIRST

All advisors are going to claim that your interests come first, whether it is true or not.

We do not want to be too cynical, but do not be overly impressed when advisors express significant interest in your goals and concerns on the telephone. There is a good chance this is a sales tactic that is designed to build a relationship with you.

At this point you are not trying to build a relationship. You are simply scheduling appointments so you can learn more about particular advisors before you select one.

SCHEDULING INTERVIEWS

At the risk of stating the obvious, you are going to have to pick a day and time to interview the advisor. Less obvious are other considerations that impact the scheduling of the interview:

- Meeting location
- Duration of the meeting
- Meeting agenda
- Type of meeting (face-to-face, virtual)

For example, you may want to schedule interviews at the advisor's location. This is one more way to gather additional information about the advisor, the advisor's staff, and the professionalism of his work environment.

If the advisor's location is too far away, you may want to select a location that is more convenient for you, such as your office, home, or a neutral location (e.g., Starbucks), or see if you can schedule a virtual interview.

Keep in mind you will want some level of privacy at the meeting location.

Ideally, the advisors will be flexible on the location, but the busier they are, the more likely they will want to meet at their location.

In the next chapter you will learn how to prepare for and conduct interviews with your candidates.

FIVE KEY TAKEAWAYS

- You may be cautious about contacting advisors due to bad experiences with aggressive salespeople.
- That concern should not apply here. You only contact pre-screened advisors you have selected for interviews.
- If you want to control the candidates, you have to be willing to initiate contact with them.
- Initial contact can be a telephone call, email, or through the advisor's website.
- You can learn more about advisors during the contact phase.

CHAPTER 7

HOW TO INTERVIEW FINANCIAL ADVISORS

As you might imagine, the interview is the most dangerous step in your advisor selection process. This is the step where you have the greatest exposure to the advisor's sales and relationship skills.

You want to select the best advisor. The advisor wants to sell you financial advice, services, and products. You make better decisions when you minimize the impact of the advisors' sales skills.

You reduce your vulnerability to sales tactics when you use a process you control to interview advisors.

The good news is you have done your homework in advance. Since you control whom you interview, you should only be talking to advisors who scored well when you researched their credentials, ethics, business practices, and services.

Your biggest challenge in this step is to maintain your objectivity while you gather additional information during the interview phase of your selection process.

Think of the interviews as your opportunity to fill in the blanks:

- Obtain information that was not published on the internet.
- Verify information that you found on the internet.
- Request clarification for any confusing information.
- Evaluate the advisors' communication skills.
- Ask for documentation for key information.

Your research should have already provided answers to many of the questions you should be asking advisors.

HOW MANY INTERVIEWS?

There are three answers to this question.

First, you want choices when you select a financial

advisor. Therefore, you should interview at least three or four advisors who successfully completed your research process.

Second, you should also interview the best advisors twice. Your goal for the initial interviews is to narrow your choice to the finalists. Then you schedule a second interview with them to check first impressions and ask additional questions.

Third, you may want to meet with the finalist a final time to discuss the details, review his service agreement, and discuss next steps. This contact is not an interview.

LOCATION OF THE INTERVIEWS

The previous chapter gave you some insight into optional locations for the interview. We recommend conducting the interviews at the advisor's office.

Most of the content in this chapter describes interviewing traditional, "brick-and-mortar" advisors. They have physical offices where you can meet with them face-to-face. This is what most investors are used to, based on their past experiences with advisors.

However, depending on your location, there can also be

consequences when you limit your options to advisors you can interview face-to-face.

WHEN LOCATION DOESN'T MATTER

You are seeking the best financial advisor, not the closest financial advisor.

You may also want to interview virtual advisors. They provide the same services as traditional advisors, but the interviews will be by telephone or a video chat service such as Skype.

There is a hidden benefit when you interview virtual advisors. You will make a more objective decision that is not impacted as much by the advisors' personality or sales skills. It is more of a direct exchange of information.

The virtual interview can include a video tour of the advisors' offices and introductions to the advisors' staff.

DURATION OF THE INTERVIEWS

You want to create a level playing field for your candidates, so each advisor should be allocated the same amount of time for their interviews. We recommend seventy-five minutes for several reasons.

This assumes you have communicated an agenda to the advisors before the interview.

It is their responsibility to follow your agenda in a timely manner.

You spend the first fifteen minutes discussing your situation, service requirements, and goals. The advisor also has the opportunity to ask questions.

The advisor spends the next forty-five minutes providing the information that is requested in your list of topics (agenda).

You spend the final fifteen minutes asking any additional questions that occurred to you during the advisor's forty-five-minute presentation.

Seventy-five minutes may seem like an odd number, but it also tells the advisors that you are serious about the amount of time each one has to provide the information you are seeking.

BACKGROUND INFORMATION

You may want to email each advisor your background information in advance, which will help them prepare for the interview. The information could include the following:

- Your current financial situation
- Your financial goals
- Your primary concerns
- Types and amounts of assets (personal, IRA, trust)
- The services you are seeking
- Your past experience with advisors
- The timing of your decision

On the other hand, you may not want to provide background information. You may obtain better information if the advisors' responses are more impromptu.

SCHEDULING INTERVIEWS

This may be a minor point, but you may want to schedule the interviews for the same day or week. Logistics and scheduling conflicts may not allow this, but the closer together you can schedule the interviews, the easier it will be to compare advisors to each other.

CONTROLLING THE INTERVIEWS

There is only one way you can control the interview, and that is to provide each advisor with an agenda that describes the information you want covered.

Then you must have the discipline to require advisors to follow the agenda.

A high percentage of advisors will attempt to deviate from the agenda. They are used to controlling interviews with their sales tactics. In fact, most advisors refer to interviews as sales presentations.

Any advisor who fails to follow the agenda should be automatically excluded from your search. The advisor did not respect your requirements for the interview.

How do you compare advisors to each other if they all have different presentations?

If you happen to interview a lower-quality advisor, keep in mind that these advisors have a lot to hide, so they will be less inclined to follow an agenda that requires them to disclose information they would rather not provide.

AGENDA ITEMS

Based on your research, you already know a lot about the financial advisors you are going to interview. Your agenda will list the remaining topics you want covered.

There are a lot of potential topics. These are some of the more important ones:

- Do they provide the services you are seeking?

- Whom will you be working with?
- What is the total expense for their advice and services?
- How is the advisor compensated?
- Are they acting in a fiduciary capacity when they provide advice?
- What is their investment philosophy and process?
- Will you receive performance reports? How frequently?
- Do they have GIPS-verified (Global Investment Performance Standard) track record?
- How often will you meet to review results?
- How do they communicate during volatile markets?

CLARITY AND VALIDATION

Your agenda should focus on information that was not available in your research of public data: advisors' websites, regulatory agencies, third-party profiles, and Google name searches.

What would you like to know that you could not find on the internet?

You may also require clarification of information that will impact your selection decision. For example, you may want to know which services are provided by the advisor versus other professionals (planning, investment, insurance, tax, legal). What is the advisor's relationship to the other professionals?

You may also want to validate information that you uncovered during the research phase. For example, you want to make sure you know who the advisor works for: himself, an RIA, a broker-dealer, a bank, or an insurance company.

We recommend you require advisors to document their responses in writing.

SENSITIVE QUESTIONS

There are no sensitive questions—not when your future financial security is impacted by the advisors' responses.

Advisors may ask you a lot of personal questions about your finances, health, profession, and retirement. You should feel equally comfortable asking personal questions that impact your selection decision.

One of the most sensitive topics is the advisors' compensation. But they derive that compensation from you and/or your assets.

Advisors can always decline to answer a particular question.

COMPENSATION

We believe this is a critical interview topic because it helps establish your expectations for that advisor. For example, an advisor whose only method of compensation is a commission is a salesperson. Therefore, you should expect to be sold investment and insurance products.

These are some typical compensation questions:

- How are you compensated?
- How much are you compensated?
- Who compensates you?
- What do I receive for the compensation?
- Is your compensation deducted from my assets?

EXPENSES

The higher the expenses, the less inclined the advisor will be to talk about them. Your interview agenda should ask some very direct questions about expenses.

As we have already described, there are layers and layers of expenses. You may be paying financial advisors, money managers, broker/dealers, and custodians when you purchase investment products such as mutual funds or exchange-traded funds.

For example, when you purchase mutual funds in your portfolio, you might pay a financial advisor a 1 percent fee for his services, which is deducted from your account and shown on your statement.

However, what you may not see are the internal (hidden) fees charged by mutual funds, such as investment management fees (1.3 percent average) and trading costs (1.4 percent average) for an additional 2.7 percent in fees (average).

These fees do not show on your statement. Rather, they are deducted from the value of your assets, so you won't necessarily notice them, except how they affect your investment performance over time.

And every dollar of expense, regardless of where it comes from, is one less dollar you have available for reinvestment.

POTENTIAL CONFLICTS OF INTEREST

There are several potential conflicts of interest that can impact your relationship with a financial advisor or firm. It is not possible to list all of them in this book, and there are new ones every month.

We can tell you that a conflict of interest occurs whenever the interests of a financial advisor or firm take precedence over doing what is best for you.

A simple illustration occurs when advisors have this choice. They could sell you Mutual Fund A (Index Fund, ETF) that produces a market rate of return for a lower fee, but also pays a lower commission. Or they could sell you Mutual Fund B, which produces a market rate of return for a higher fee, but pays a bigger commission.

Assuming you have a lower tolerance for risk, a conflict of interest occurs when the advisor recommends Mutual Fund B. You pay a higher fee so the advisor can earn a bigger commission. This happens thousands of time per day, and most investors do not know it is happening because they were never presented with a choice or this level of disclosure.

You can try to minimize the impact of conflicts of interest by asking questions during the interview and requiring documented responses before or after the interview.

Here are some example questions:

- Are you a financial fiduciary? Will you acknowledge that in writing?
- Are you legally required to always act in my best interests?
- Do you practice full disclosure for all relevant information?
- Will you disclose any potential conflicts of interest?
- Does the firm you work for have any potential conflicts of interest?
- Will you be selling me proprietary products?
- Will I always have investment choices?
- Do you recommend low-cost solutions even if you make less money?

The answers for most of these questions can also be found in the advisor's Form ADV. Even if the same information is available in the Form ADV, you should ask the questions to verify, to clarify, and to see if any of his answers deviate from the information in the ADV.

PLANNING PROCESS

Financial plans are produced by software and the application of the financial professional's expertise. It is a good idea to ask questions about the sophistication of the advisor's planning services:

- Do you develop basic financial plans or more sophisticated retirement and estate plans?
- Do your plans recommend the purchase of specific financial products? (mutual funds, annuities, or long-term care insurance)
- How frequently do you update the plan, and what does it cost to do that?
- How do I pay for a financial plan? Is it a separate fee or bundled with an investment fee?
- Do you provide fee-only financial planning?
- Will you produce a financial plan without investing my assets or selling me a product?

There is software that turns out cookie-cutter plans and software that produces sophisticated, custom-tailored plans.

Some software is designed to sell investment and insurance products.

INVESTMENT PROCESS

Similar to planning, you should learn more about the advisor's investment processes during the interview:

- What types of investments do you recommend? (e.g., securities, mutual funds, ETFs, insurance products)
- How do you allocate my money into the various asset classes?

- Do you provide an Investment Policy Statement as one of your core services?
- How do you manage risk in rising, flat, and falling markets?
- Who does your investment research?
- Who makes the investment decisions for my assets?
- Do I have online access to my investment data?
- Do I have to approve investment decisions before they are implemented?
- Will I receive monthly or quarterly performance reports?

TRACK RECORDS

When it comes to choosing someone to make decisions with your money, nothing serves as better verification of ability than the truth about a financial advisor's past performance.

A logical question to ask in an interview is "What are realistic performance expectations?" or "What rate of return should I expect if I select you as my advisor?"

Many advisors will say they've created good results, but when it comes to the "show me the numbers" moment, they can't produce any concrete evidence in writing.

Advisors build financial plans and invest your portfolio

accordingly. In cases where portfolios are customized for each client, advisors will say that there is no track record because each portfolio is different. For example, the investments for a thirty-five-year-old are likely to be more aggressive than those for an eighty-year-old couple. The portfolios are going to be invested differently—but nonetheless, there should be a track record for each type.

Any performance information that is provided by an advisor must be documented.

MUST BE VERIFIED

You can ask for track records during the interviews, but most advisors will not be able to provide one—at least not a legitimate one that is GIPS compliant and audited by an accredited third party.

You can learn more about GIPS and see a list of all firms claiming compliance at www.gipsstandards.org. Check this website for confirmation when speaking with any financial advisor who says that he or she follows these standards. All the top advisors and money managers are on this list.

Any firm can claim GIPS compliance, but this must be verified by a third party if you want to trust the results. The top-performing GIPS-verification firms are ACA Compliance (www.acacompliancegroup. com) and Spaulding Group (www.spauldinggrp.com). The "Big Four" accounting firms (Deloitte, PwC, Ernst & Young, and KPMG) render these services as well. Unless a reputable firm such as these have placed their stamp of approval on a firm's track record, there is no way to know if the advisor is truly GIPS compliant.

When institutions (corporate pension plan) select advisors, they require a GIPS-verified track record.

The small percentage of advisors who can document valid track records should have a significant advantage in your selection process. They went to a lot of expense to document the performance of their current clients. They also demonstrate a higher level of transparency and accountability in providing their verified track records.

Any advisor who provides verbal performance numbers during an interview should be automatically excluded from your selection process. How do you trust advisors who use this deceptive sales tactic?

PAST PERFORMANCE NO GUARANTEE OF FUTURE RESULTS

Every advisor's and money manager's track record has the following disclaimer for a reason: "Past performance does not guarantee future results." In fact, there may little to no relationship between past and future performance. Market conditions keep changing to reflect changes in the economy (interest rates, inflation, GDP) and company outlooks (revenue growth, earnings). But being able to show verified past performance is a better future indicator than showing no performance at all.

OTHER BUSINESS PRACTICES

These are some additional questions that could be asked during the interview:

- Do you provide tax and legal advice (if applicable)?
- Am I a big or small client for you?
- Who is my principal contact? The advisor? An associate?
- What is the frequency of our communications?
- How will we communicate? (e.g., reports, meetings, calls)
- How accessible are you in an urgent situation?
- Do you provide services to individuals, institutions, or both?

- Who is the backup if my key contact is not available?

DOCUMENTATION

Interviews, by their very nature, are verbal, but that does not mean the advisor should not document his verbal representations.

At the risk of being repetitious, we strongly recommend that you trust what you see and not what you hear when you interview financial advisors.

The simple fact is verbal information is too easy to manipulate. More importantly, you have no record of what was said to you. Here are some examples of information that should be documented:

- Fee schedules
- Service agreements
- Fiduciary acknowledgment
- Compensation arrangement
- Combined expenses
- Track records

PROOF STATEMENTS (SAMPLES)

You should ask for samples of the advisor's work as part

of your interview process. An advisor who provides you with samples of real work will remove the client's name to protect his privacy.

One sample could be an actual financial plan:

- What software was used to prepare the plan?
- How comprehensive is the plan?
- How sophisticated is the plan?
- Does the plan look like a service that would benefit you?

Another sample is an actual portfolio:

- How were the assets invested? (e.g., securities, mutual funds, ETFs)
- How were the assets allocated?
- Does the portfolio look like a service that would benefit you?

REFERENCES

You already know references are easy to manipulate and that no advisor will give you a bad reference, so this really limits their value.

It is smart to assume that references, who might include current clients and other professionals (CPAs, attorneys), have personal relationships with the advisors. Some references may have even been coached to make sure their comments match what was said to you by advisors.

The best references would be former clients who have terminated the advisor's services.

Regardless of value or objectivity, advisors should be prepared to provide references if you ask for them. You should also be able to obtain the following information from the references:

- Is the reference's situation similar to yours?
- How long have they been a client?
- What services do they receive?
- What does the reference like most about the advisor?
- What does the reference like least about the advisor?
- What were your expectations for the advisor?

As discussed earlier, references are not a substitute for track records.

Why spend time talking to references? It might make you feel more comfortable about selecting a particular advisor.

THE BIG QUESTION

After getting all of your questions answered and filling in the gaps of your research, you should know everything you need to know about the advisors. But there is one remaining question that you should always ask: "Why should I select you or your firm versus a competitor?"

There is lot of value in this open-ended question:

- Did the advisor read your situation properly?
- Has he identified with you as a potential client?
- How does he differentiate himself from other advisors?
- Is the response a sales pitch or specific features and benefits?
- What is his value proposition?

FINAL INTERVIEW

You may have a clear winner after the first interview. This is okay if you believe you have enough information to select the best advisor for the right reasons.

On the other hand, you may want a second interview for the finalists to check your first impressions.

This is an important step if you still have not identified a clear winner.

To break the tie, you will need to develop some specific questions that are important to you—perhaps even questions that are unique to your situation. For example, you are going to retire in twelve months and are concerned about stock market volatility.

FIVE KEY TAKEAWAYS

- You have to control the agenda so advisors provide the same information.
- Advisors who try to control the agenda are automatically excluded.
- You have to minimize the impact of advisor sales skills and personalities.
- You should have all the information you need to select the two finalists.
- Your last step is the interview that selects the winner.

CHAPTER 8

HOW TO SELECT THE BEST FINANCIAL ADVISOR

At this point a lot of information is flying around inside your head. You have learned a lot about financial advisors and a proven way for selecting the best financial advisor. Now it is time to apply the information and make the right decision.

We know many investors prefer to keep the process simple by selecting the advisor they like the best or the one with the best sales pitch. But by now you should know that is a very risky way to select an advisor who will influence or control your financial decisions.

Your key to selecting the best advisor is an objective process. Then your decision is based on factual information that you know is true. Only high-quality advisors should make it through your process.

Best case, you will identify one advisor who stands out above all the rest or two advisors who are equally qualified and it doesn't really matter which one you select.

If you have reduced several choices down to two excellent candidates, you have done a great job finding, researching, and interviewing financial advisors.

In case you are still not convinced, we are going to take one more shot at convincing you that mistakes can produce disastrous financial consequences:

- It could be years before you know you made a mistake.
- You could pay thousands of dollars of excess fees.
- You could be exposed to unnecessary risk.
- Your assets may underperform relative to benchmarks and indices.
- You may be forced to defer your retirement or reduce your standard of living during retirement.

You are reading this book for a reason. You want to increase the probability that you select the best advisor.

This chapter was written to help you make the right decision.

We can provide background information and an objective process. You have to make the selection decision.

REVIEW THE FACTS

The foundation of your selection decision should be factual information that includes educational background, years of experience, quality certifications, and clean compliance records. Hopefully, you know what all of this means by now.

You accumulated this factual information during the research phase. Any verbal information you received during the interview phase should be documented and verified to the best of your ability. For example, if the advisor says he holds a CFA designation, you should go to the CFA Institute website and verify that the designation is current.

Again, to be safe, you should discount verbal information that was not documented by the advisors. Too often, this information is part of a finely honed sales pitch.

Without question, the accuracy of advisor information increases when it is documented.

ADD SOME INTUITION

If you have one superior candidate, you should choose that advisor.

If you have two superior candidates, you can use your intuition to break the tie. Which one would you be most comfortable working with?

You have done your homework, so at this point a little subjectivity is OK as long as the professionals are equally qualified to be your advisor.

A major risk is letting subjectivity creep into your decision-making simply because you like the advisor. You may even be inclined to forgo the research process because you like a particular advisor. This is a major source of risk if you select the advisor with the best personality or sales skills versus the advisor with the best qualifications.

It is important to note that the best advisor may not be the most personable advisor. There are a lot of numbers and analysis in the financial advice business, so the best advisors may be intellectual, quantitative, and analytical. You might even classify them as nerds. You may not want to play a round of golf with them, but they are excellent financial advisors.

COMPARING ADVISORS

We know you want to select the best financial advisor. So your objective process should include a way to compare advisors to each other.

You may want to consider a spreadsheet that enables you to array their information side by side. For example, you have four high-quality finalists, and you are struggling to determine which one to select.

You can array certain characteristics side by side in a way that makes it easier to compare and rate the advisors. For example, you can have the following rows of information:

- Years of experience
- Education
- Certifications
- Fiduciary status
- Compliance records
- Method(s) of compensation
- GIPS-verified track records (if they have one)

You may want to weight some of the responses so they have more impact in your selection process. For example, you may feel experience is more important than education, so you might give experience a weighting of 1.5 and education a weighting of 1.0. You can apply any weightings that work for you.

If ethics are your number-one priority, the weighting could be 2.0 because trustworthiness is more important than competence. What good is advice if you can't trust it?

You could even create a weighting factor for your subjectivity. A neutral weighting could be 1.0, indicating you do not have strong feelings one way or the other. Someone you might look forward to working with could receive a weighting of 1.5. Someone you might not look forward to working with receives a 0.5. In this category, someone you liked scored three times higher than someone you did not particularly care for. In addition, the advisor with the 0.5 likeability rating will have to score very high in other categories to overcome the low score that reflects your intuitive feelings about working with him.

The advisors with the highest scores are your finalists.

ONLINE RATING SERVICE

You can also use the free, no-registration-required advisor rating tool on the Paladin Registry website (www.PaladinRegistry.com) to help you make the right decision. Go to "Rate a Financial Advisor" under "Investor Tools."

After answering ten questions about each advisor, the

Paladin service uses a proprietary algorithm to calculate the advisors' ratings (1–5 stars). This is an easy way to compare advisor qualifications.

TIEBREAKERS

If you have trouble determining which professional you should select, answer the following questions to break the tie and make the right decision.

- Which advisor had the best qualifications: credentials, ethics, business practices?
- Who do you think is the most trustworthy based on licensing, employment, and compliance record?
- Which advisor was the most transparent, providing factual information without being asked?
- Which advisor had the best communication skills? (verbal and written)
- Which advisor has the most experience working with clients who are similar to you?
- Which advisor asked the best questions about your current situation?
- Which advisor provided the best, most complete answers to your questions?
- Which advisor seemed more inclined to educate you along the way so you can make increasingly informed decisions?

- If you are married, which advisor recommended including your spouse in the interview?
- Which advisor promised the best ongoing services? (e.g., meetings, reports, reviews, calls, emails, etc.)

Your research and interviews should have uncovered the answers to many of these questions.

ADVISOR SERVICE AGREEMENT

There is one more step after you make your selection decision. You will have to sign the advisor's service agreement and additional documents that the advisor needs to move your assets to his broker/dealer or custodian.

It has been our experience that 75 percent of investors do not read these documents before they sign them. If they did, they might be surprised by content that has two primary purposes—to provide required disclosures and to protect the firm that is providing the advice and services.

Why spend time reading the agreement? After all, you trusted the advisor enough to select him.

It is a major mistake not to read the agreement. The advisor's agreement can include a series of conditions, disclosures, disclaimers, limitations, and procedures that may make you very uncomfortable.

Advisors use sales tactics to get you to buy. For example, they tell you what you want to hear. The agreement describes the real conditions of the relationship, but you won't know that if you don't read it.

As we have said more than once, when your money is at stake, trust what you see and not what you hear.

Be extra cautious if the agreement is long, printed in small font, or loaded with legal language. At some point you may even feel a need to have an attorney review the document or someone who is familiar with these types of service agreements.

Any open issues should be negotiated in advance and added as addendums to the document. You may find some advisory firms do not like addendums that protect you.

Following are five types of content that you want documented in the agreement:

- Who employs or licenses the advisor, and who owns the firm? There may be layers of ownership.
- Is the financial advisor acting in a fiduciary capacity

when he provides financial advice and services? Is there written acknowledgment in the agreement?

- Is the advisor's fee schedule published in the agreement? Are the payments in advance or arrears?
- Which firm (custodian) has physical possession of your assets?
- How do you terminate the agreement?

A service agreement sounds more benign than a contract, but it is binding. Read it before you sign it.

EXPECTATIONS

Some financial advisors create high expectations to convince you to buy what they are selling. Commission sales representatives are prone to do this because they are paid at the time of sale, and there are no financial consequences if they fail to meet the expectations they created.

Fee advisors are less prone to create high expectations because they can be terminated if they do not meet the expectations they created in the interviews. This is one more reason why you should select an advisor who is compensated with fees.

Watch out for high expectations that are sales ploys. You

want realistic expectations that have a high probability of occurring.

Financial promises and guarantees for future results are illegal. That's because no one has a crystal ball that can predict the future. Any advisors who promise or guarantee particular results or outcomes should be automatically excluded from your selection process.

Once you agree on a realistic set of expectations, you should document them in writing. Down the road— one, two, or three years later—it is going to be difficult to remember exactly what you were told to expect.

When it is time to remember what they told you, some advisors develop a short-term condition that is known as selective amnesia. They only remember information that benefits them.

ACCOUNTABILITY

Advisors do not like accountability because it can cause you to terminate their services.

However, your agreement should include accountability so your advisor knows not only what is expected, but also the consequences of his failure to meet your expectations.

Expectations and accountability should be spelled out in your agreement with the advisor. This may be an addendum to the advisor's agreement.

Expectations and accountability are the foundation of your relationship with a financial advisor.

THE END

We hope our time-tested, objective process helped you select a trustworthy expert who can help you make your financial future a secure, comfortable one.

TOP FIVE TAKEAWAYS

- Factual information is the foundation of your selection process.
- Use your intuition when you are down to two equally qualified advisors.
- Advisors create expectations when they sell their advice and services.
- Make sure you read the service agreement before you sign it.
- Advisors must be held accountable for the expectations that they create.

CHAPTER 9

AVOID ADVISOR BLINDSIDES

The focus of this book is describing how you can use the internet to make better decisions when you select financial advisors.

Or, taken a step further, the book describes how to use the internet to protect your financial interests.

We would be remiss if we did not include a chapter that also describes how you can use the internet to monitor your advisor to make sure there are no surprises that could damage your financial security.

We titled this chapter "Avoid Advisor Blindsides" because millions of investors have experienced blindsides (surprises) after they've selected their advisors. Something they did not know or expect damaged them, and they did not see it coming.

The most dangerous advisor in America is a likeable professional who is trustworthy at the beginning of a relationship but, for any number of reasons, becomes untrustworthy later in the relationship. It could be one year, five years, or ten years later.

Blindsides occur when someone you trust takes advantage of you to make more money from your assets.

The information in this chapter will help you use the internet to monitor a current advisor who is influencing or controlling your financial decisions.

Monitoring is the early warning system that protects your financial interests.

WHY IS THIS CHAPTER IMPORTANT?

Your goal is to select a competent, ethical advisor. Your research determines which advisors you are going to interview and eventually the advisor you are going to select.

- You may like your new advisor.

- You may trust your new advisor.
- You still have to monitor your new advisor.
- No surprises!

You hope you selected the right advisor, but it can take years before you know if you made the right decision. In fact, it may take a severe market decline before you know how good your advisor really is. Everyone looks like a genius in a bull market.

Every year, millions of investors acknowledge that they selected the wrong professional when they fire their current financial advisors.

EXTERNAL EVENTS

As you will see in this chapter, your relationship with an advisor can be impacted by serious events that are outside the relationship. Perhaps the advisor did not meet your expectations for investment performance. However, it is also likely that an ethical breach was caused by outside events that created a need for the advisor to make more money from your assets.

Why would an advisor do that? Read on.

THIS RISK IS REAL

It stands to reason that there will always be a small percentage of advisors who let their need for money overwhelm their responsibility to do what is best for you.

How big is the problem? In 2016, FINRA reported 1,434 disciplinary actions that resulted in the suspension or banning of more than 1,200 financial advisors from the industry—temporarily or permanently.

This is the tip of a very big iceberg. There are millions of other investors who have been damaged, but chose not to file complaints. They just fired the advisors who damaged them and selected new advisors.

How real are the risks?

This type of damage occurs after you select an advisor. Therein lies your number-one reason for monitoring your current advisor.

ETHICS VS. COMPETENCE

Again, we hope we are not being too cynical, but we believe a significant percentage of the financial service representatives will take advantage of clients to produce increased revenue for companies and income for themselves. You have seen the headlines. The biggest financial firms in America have paid billions of dollars of fines for cheating their clients.

Taking advantage of you to make more money is an ethical issue.

There is also a competence issue. It could be that the advisor who represented himself as a financial expert is actually new to the industry. Misrepresentation is an ethical issue, but you may have been damaged by the advisor's lack of knowledge that resulted in bad advice.

Ethical lapses and lack of competence are hidden risks—the two main reasons why you should monitor your current financial advisor.

EVENTS THAT IMPACT ADVISORS

In the beginning of the relationship, advisors are doing what is best for you. Later in the relationship, they may start taking advantage of the relationship to make more money.

This could have been their intent all along—establish trust, then use it to make more money. Or perhaps an event occurred that created a need for more money.

Following are a few examples of events that can impact the lives of advisors and put you at risk:

- Your advisor is filing for personal bankruptcy.
- Your advisor is losing a home in a foreclosure.
- Your advisor is getting a divorce (legal fees, alimony, child support).
- Your advisor is being overwhelmed by personal debt.
- Your advisor is impacted by an expensive, major health issue (or a family member).
- Your advisor is impacted by personal investment losses.
- Your advisor is sued by the IRS.
- Your advisor is sued by other clients.
- Your advisor is funding another business that is in trouble.

In every situation, the problem could be solved with more money. The easiest way an unscrupulous advisor can make more money is to take advantage of existing relationships.

You rarely see it coming when someone you like and trust takes advantage of you—the blindside.

If you live in Seattle, you could have made the mistake of selecting Mark Spangler. He had exceptional credentials and no disclosures on his compliance record prior to defrauding his clients out of more than $30 million. Many of these investors were smart, successful employees of Microsoft.

Like Bernie Madoff, he used his affiliation with a nationally recognized organization to gain the trust of his clients. But then his world changed. He needed quick capital to keep his side business afloat—in this case, a high-tech start-up company. His solution was a Ponzi scheme that blindsided his clients.

He is currently serving a fifteen-year prison sentence.

SOURCES OF DATA

Some investors allow their advisors to monitor themselves, which is like letting the fox guard the hen house. If your advisor is able to control what you do and do not see, it is safe to assume that he will provide the information that keeps him retained and withhold information that could get him fired.

Fortunately, you have tools and a process for monitoring your advisor. As easy as it was to use the methods outlined in this book to research an advisor, it will be just as easy to use the tools to monitor a current advisor.

You just need a process for gathering information and the discipline to review the information on a regular basis.

For example, you may receive a monthly or quarterly performance measurement report from your financial advisor. The information in the report helps you measure the quality of the advice you are being given. You just have to know what you are looking at.

Bernie Madoff manufactured fake reports to perpetuate his Ponzi scheme.

Then there is the data that is not provided by your advisor. For example, you can use the internet to monitor events by entering the advisor's name and the advisor firm's name in Google with additional keywords such as "fraud," "lawsuit," "IRS," "FINRA," "SEC," "fine," and so on.

MONITORING YOUR EXPECTATIONS

You already know that advisors create expectations during interviews to gain control of your assets. This is part of their sales process—telling you what you can expect if you select them.

You should develop a system for monitoring expectations that you can use to compare what you were told to expect versus your actual experience.

For example, an advisor tells you he will protect the market value of your investments during a down market. Did that actually happen?

Or the advisor tells you he will meet with you face-to-face on a quarterly basis to review your results. Did that actually happen? Or did you have to make several requests to schedule a review session?

How long do you give advisors to meet expectations? Advisors generally like to have three years to perform under a variety of market conditions. You may have a shorter fuse than that.

THE BLAME GAME

A healthy relationship occurs when you and your advisor agree, in writing, how he is going to be accountable for his advice, services, and results.

Now you have something to monitor.

But watch out for excuses. Many advisors are prone to blaming others or things they can't control for their lack of results. They dodge accountability by blaming falling stock prices, rising interest rates, increasing inflation, government policy, and so on.

Part of their expertise should be to invest your assets in a variety of market conditions.

You are monitoring your results. You know there is a problem. The question is: Do you let the advisor's blame game buy time, or do you terminate the relationship because the advisor did not meet expectations?

Excuses should not diminish the advisor's accountability.

MONITORING EXPENSES

Monitoring performance should be at the top of your list. Monitoring expenses that are deducted from your accounts should be a close second. You may find there are layers and layers of fees that are being deducted from your assets.

You do not want to be blindsided years later when you fail to achieve your financial goals due to excessive expenses.

Expenses are deducted from your assets so you do not have to take any action to pay industry fees, commissions, and transaction charges. This way, there are no accounts receivable problems in the financial service industry.

You would be much more aware of expenses if you

had to write a check or use a debit card. Wall Street wants to minimize your awareness for expenses.

Most professionals and firms bill quarterly in arrears. In other words, they deliver the service, then they bill your account. Some firms bill in quarterly advance, so you pay for the service before you receive it. You should know the difference.

Some of the worst investment products have the highest expenses so they can pay big commissions that incentivize advisors to sell some really bad products.

You already know about the several layers of expense from a previous chapter.

Financial advisory firms pass all of these expenses through to you.

MONITORING TRADES

You should have online access to your account information. We recommend using the internet to monitor the trading activity in your accounts—what is being bought and what is being sold, and the frequency of that turnover.

There can be too much activity, the right amount of

activity, or a lack of activity. Higher activity or turnover is generally thought to be problematic. Lower activity may be a problem if your portfolio is underperforming.

Examples of potential trading problems include the following:

- Churning (excessive turnover)
- Buy high, sell low
- Inconsistency with your objectives
- Too much or too little diversification
- Unauthorized trading

COMPLIANCE RECORD

Registered Investment Advisors are supposed to send their clients an updated ADV every year, which should include any changes to their compliance record. You can use the internet to monitor your advisor's compliance record at www.adviserinfo.sec.gov or www.brokercheck.finra.org.

Schedule a periodic review on your calendar so you don't forget.

You are looking for changes in the advisor's disciplinary record, registrations, firm affiliations, or other public disclosures, such as bankruptcies, tax liens, or criminal activities.

How soon would you want to know about a change that creates concern and increased risk for you? Monitoring should be quarterly, semi-annually, or annually. Your level of concern about this issue should determine the frequency.

BETTER BUSINESS BUREAU

A periodic check of the BBB's database is a good idea. Enter your advisor's name and the advisor's firm name to check for any new complaints or comments.

GOOGLE NAME SEARCHES

Google name searches should be conducted periodically to look for information that your advisor has not disclosed to you.

As noted earlier, you can combine the advisor's name and the advisor's firm name with various keywords that will help you find the information you are seeking (e.g., "news," "lawsuit," "criminal," "fraud," "complaint," "fine," etc.).

LOCAL PRESS

Do not overlook your local newspaper. There may be information in the online version of the newspaper that is cause for concern. For example, most newspapers report on local financial scams and other types of activities that may damage their readers.

Use the same process as the Google name search to find information in the local press.

ONLINE ACCOUNT DATA

Your advisor should provide online access to your account data. You can use your access to monitor performance, expenses, transactions, and other data that impacts your financial results.

CONFRONTATION

You may be reluctant to confront your advisor with accusations about his competence, ethics, or results. This is particularly true if you consider the advisor a friend.

This is an excellent reason for not making your advisor a friend—you can be more objective when you review his advice, services, expenses, and results.

The simplest solution to avoid confrontation is to terminate your advisor and find a new one. But is this the best solution? You should give the current advisor the opportunity to address your concerns.

It is not confrontation; it is your right because it is your money and your financial future that is at stake.

CHANGING ADVISORS

Terminating an advisor usually means you have lost time and money in your quest to accumulate more assets for retirement. A higher-quality advisor would have produced more assets during that time period.

Changing advisors should not be taken lightly. It may be the easiest decision, but it is not necessarily the right decision. There is no guarantee that the new advisor will be better than the terminated advisor, in particular if you use the same selection process.

The only thing more damaging than selecting the wrong advisor is to continue your relationship with the wrong advisor.

The sooner you identify a problem, the sooner you can take action. That is why we recommend that you monitor your current advisor.

It is your financial future that is at stake. If you are going to allow an advisor to influence or control your financial decisions, you had better be very certain that you selected the right professional or firm.

FIVE KEY TAKEAWAYS

- Good advisors become bad advisors when they take advantage of clients to make more money.
- A change in an advisor's financial circumstances can impact clients.
- Regulatory agencies get involved after the fact, when your money may be gone.
- Monitoring advisors is the best way to avoid being blindsided by incompetent and/or unethical advisors.
- Monitoring is your early warning system.

CHAPTER 10

HOW YOU WIN
THE GAME

We wrote this book for four reasons:

- To show you how to use the internet to find, research, and contact financial advisors
- To provide a process that enables you to control your selection decision
- To help you win the game (select the best financial advisor)
- To reduce your risk of losing the game (select a low-quality advisor)

We hope you read every chapter. But if you only read one chapter, make it this one. It tells you what to look for when you select a financial advisor.

THE GAME

You want financial security during your working years, retirement years, and late in life when you need it the most.

You need a competent, ethical financial advisor who can help you achieve these goals.

Selecting the right professional is complicated because many advisors do not have the specialized knowledge that will help you achieve your goals. They make their living selling investment and insurance products.

Real financial experts are more rare. We estimate they are at most 25 percent of the advisors who market financial advice and services.

It is you versus the financial service industry.

HOW YOU WIN

You must control the selection process to win the game.

The internet is your key to winning the game. You can use it for the following:

- Find financial advisors who meet your specific requirements.

- Research advisor credentials and ethics.
- Contact the advisors you want to interview.
- Make decisions based on factual information.
- Select the best financial advisor.
- Monitor current advisors.

The internet has changed the way you buy goods and services. Now it is changing the way you select a financial advisor.

TAKING THE INITIATIVE

The internet is a game changer, but only if you take the initiative. For example, you use the internet to find, research, and contact financial advisors.

If you don't take the initiative, you are leaving it up to advisors to initiate contact with you.

If that happens, you lose control over the process and increase the risk that you will select the advisor with the best sales skills instead of the one who is most competent.

WHO ARE THE BEST FINANCIAL ADVISORS?

Any competent, ethical financial professional who puts your interests first could be considered the best advisor.

You can use the five steps (Find, Research, Contact, Interview, and Select) in this book to help you implement a process that helps you pick the best financial advisor.

The rest of this final chapter will describe the top ten characteristics that you should be seeking when you select a financial advisor.

I. RIAS AND IARS

You should limit your selection to Registered Investment Advisors (firms) and Investment Advisor Representatives (professionals).

These registrations permit professionals and firms to provide financial advice and ongoing services for fees.

Tip: Make sure the professional acknowledges this registration in his service agreement.

2. FINANCIAL FIDUCIARY

A fiduciary is a firm or person who holds a position of trust.

Who holds a more important position of trust than a financial advisor who will impact when you retire, how you live during retirement, and your financial security late in life when you need it the most?

Many investors believe being a fiduciary is the most important financial advisor characteristic. Fiduciaries are held to the highest ethical standards in the financial service industry.

Only RIAs and IARs are financial fiduciaries.

Tip: You must select a fiduciary advisor if you want a professional who is "required" to put your financial interests first.

3. RECORD OF COMPLIANCE

Who do you trust with your financial future?

It should be a financial advisor with a clean compliance record. Or, if there is a blemish, it was a frivolous complaint that was rejected by a regulatory agency.

Tip: The best financial advisors have a history of following the rules.

4. FINANCIAL EXPERTISE

Only select an advisor who can prove he is a real financial expert based on relevant education, experience, and certifications. This information should be documented for your records.

Tip: The best advisors have years of applicable experience providing advice and services to clients like you.

5. TRANSPARENCY

High-quality advisors volunteer the information you need to make the right selection decision. They do not withhold information, because they have nothing to hide.

Tip: Be very cautious if you have to dig for information.

6. COMPENSATION

The best financial advisors are compensated with fees just like the other professionals (CPAs, attorneys) you depend on for specialized advice and services.

Tip: Your preferred method of payment for financial advice and services should be one of the three types of fees that are charged by advisors (hourly, fixed, asset-based).

7. EXPENSES

The advisor's compensation is an expense. There can also be layers of additional expenses. The best financial advisors will fully disclose all of the expenses that will be deducted from your accounts.

Tip: The trustworthiness of financial advisors goes up when they disclose expenses, who gets the money, and what you receive in return.

8. TRACK RECORDS

Financial advisors know you have performance expectations when you select them. The best advisors provide documentation for their historical returns that are based on industry-accepted methodologies.

Tip: You should not rely on verbal performance numbers from advisors and references.

9. COMMUNICATION

The best financial advisors provide the information you need to get a good night's sleep. They provide a blend of reports, meetings, emails, and calls to keep you fully informed about the performance of your assets.

Tip: A quarterly performance report that explains your results is the most important type of written communication.

10. FINANCIAL SERVICES

The best advisors provide wealth-related advice and services and have access to the resources and expertise in all of the financial planning disciplines—planning, investment, insurance, tax, and legal—to help you achieve your financial goals.

Tip: The best advisors provide advice and services. They do not sell products.

WHAT DO YOU WIN?

How much do you win if you select the best financial advisor?

How about $1 million?

Small improvements in results can have a big impact on your ability to accumulate assets for retirement. For example, Vanguard, the largest no-load mutual fund family in America, conducted a study that found high-quality financial advisors can improve your investment results by as much as 3 percent annually.

When you compound a 3 percent improvement over a longtime period, the results may astound you. It can be worth in excess of $1 million if the compounding period is long enough. Imagine how an additional $1 million could impact your standard of living during your retirement years.

Rising longevity increases your need for additional retirement assets.

This is why choosing the right advisor is the most important financial decision you will ever make. It is not as dramatic as winning the lottery, but it can definitely impact how you live in the future.

TOP FIVE TAKEAWAYS

These final tips summarize why the content in this book can change your financial life:

- The internet is a game changer. It gives you access to the information you need to research financial advisor credentials, ethics, business practices, and services.
- You have to control the process if you want to select the best financial advisor.
- You have to minimize the impact of financial advisor personalities and sales skills on your selection decision.
- Your final selection decision should be based on factual information that you have been able to verify.
- The best advisors have the ten characteristics that are described in this chapter.

ABOUT THE AUTHORS

JACK WAYMIRE, author of *Who's Watching Your Money?*, spent twenty-eight years in the financial service industry. He left the industry in 2004 to develop PaladinRegistry.com, a free website that has educated millions of investors about financial advisors and matched thousands of investors to vetted advisors in their communities.

JONATHAN DASH is the Founder and Chief Investment Officer of Dash Investments, an independent investment advisory firm. With more than twenty years of experience in investment management, he has an established reputation as a superior money manager. Dash Investments has been covered in major business publications such as *Barron's*, the *Wall Street Journal*, and the *New York Times*.

INDEX